CLOWN TOWN

BY

LOU MACALUSO

First published by Dog Ear Publishing
4010 W. 86th Street, Ste H
Indianapolis, IN 46268
www.dogearpublishing.net

ISBN: 978-159858-637-4

This book is printed on acid-free paper.

Printed in the United States of America

This is a memoir.
There are no lies,
Only memories.
Memories are events
Seasoned with time's
Unique spices:
Imagination,
Exaggeration,
And color.

—The author

The fear of death follows from the fear of life.

A man who lives fully is prepared to die at any time.

—**Mark Twain**

Prologue

Sunday, 3:15 a.m.

My wife, Dorinda, hates the sound of a ringing phone, especially when we're asleep, so the ringer is turned off on our bedroom telephone. I hear it in the next room, and instinctively I sit up and pivot my body so that my feet land on the cool hardwood floor. My hands feel my way through the thick darkness, and I hope that I don't step on one of the four sleeping dogs on my way to it. The answering machine is set to engage after the fourth ring, and I have invented this obsessive game of answering the phone before then.

I win again. Before I put the receiver to my ear, however, I realize the time. Good news doesn't come at 3:15 a.m. The best I can hope for is that some drunk left a bar on Western Avenue in our southside Chicago neighborhood and drank enough courage to call an ex-girlfriend; maybe ours is one of the many wrong numbers he will call tonight.

No such luck. It's my brother-in-law, Wayne. I can hear my sister, Beth, crying in the background.

"The hospital called. Your mom's had a bad night. She's on life support. There's no hurry now, but we need to get there and make a decision."

It was the phone call we had dreaded but knew was coming.

After a brief conversation with Wayne, I lumber to the doorway of our bedroom and peer through the darkness. Dorinda is sitting up.

"What is it?" she asks in a way that tells me that she really already knew.

"The Cardinal's in trouble," I answer. How stupid, I think! Even at a sober moment like death, I find it necessary to joke. We gave Mom that nickname because of her fascination and love of that red bird.

The hospital is less than a mile away. It'll take some time for my sisters, Terri and Beth who live in distant suburbs of Chicago to get there, so I tell Dorinda that there's no need to rush.

Before getting dressed I wander down to my sanctuary, the basement bar. For some reason the darkness comforts me. My bare feet carefully find my way to the finished basement. The bright streetlights stream through the unshaded windows and softly illuminate the bar area.

I think, what would Big Lou do now? The answer comes immediately. I follow my father's lead and pour myself a shot of some darkish booze, even though I'm not partial to hard liquor. I carry my drink to the front of the bar and seat myself comfortably on the cushioned oak stool.

Now settled and alone with my thoughts, I stare blankly into the semi-darkness. A sadness overwhelms me as my eyes begin to well. Almost as a reflex, I stop the process. I close my eyes tightly and try to control my thoughts. Something funny! Yes! Think of something humorous and I'll be fine!

Why do I do this? Why do I find it necessary to suppress uncomfortable thoughts? Do I always have to make jokes or clown around just to get through situations? Where did this come from?

A ridiculous image emerges which makes me snicker. It's a black-and-white vision of Orson Welles but with my head. The head turns and tries to mutter, "Rosebud," but instead the words come out, "Clown Town."

Chapter 1

"Eighteen grand is pretty steep for this place." Big Lou scowled at the agent, a preppy-looking guy about twenty-four-years-old with a closely cropped crew-cut and black-rimmed glasses.

Big Lou was only thirty and seemed much older and wiser than the agent. Even though my dad was short, people often referred to him as "Big Lou" just from the way he carried himself. With his stocky build, jet-black curly hair, and noticeable limp from a World War II injury, he commanded attention whenever he approached people. Emotionally, he was a complicated man. Laughter or shouting would burst from him, but only after extreme efforts to hide or to control himself. His usual facial expression was that of an introspective scowl.

"Let's go back inside and talk about it," the agent suggested.

My father gave my mother a look that meant, "Stay out here while I talk business."

She turned away with a bit of a frown. She was the dutiful young housewife of the 1950s. She was also a smart businesswoman who had been successful selling jewelry for several years prior to her marriage.

Mom's small green eyes, thin lips and nose, round face, and curvy figure presented a cute young woman. Slightly shorter than my dad, she was known for her perfect posture and quick nervous movements. She must have been wearing her favorite dress, a green-and-white-striped cotton summer shift that complimented her figure. The antithesis of my father, my mother laughed, cried, and shouted unselfconsciously.

"Keep an eye on your brother!" Mom yelled at my older sister, Beth, as she and I raced up and down the lane, a double sidewalk that separated the houses.

Mom folded her arms, dropped her head in thought, and walked toward the back of the house. Along the hedges that separated the backyard from the neighbors, strips of fertile black soil teased her yearning to have her own garden. A freshly painted white picket fence bordered the backyard.

Across the alleyway, another picket fence bordered a neighboring backyard. An attractive red-haired young woman was hanging clothes on a clothesline while her toddler son played in a sandbox near the house.

"That's what I should be doing!" Mom shouted and smiled as she approached the picket fence.

"Ha' there! Movin' in are ya'?" The accent hinted at her Mississippi roots.

"Don't know yet. What do you think? Would that be a good idea?"

"Well, we like it here," responded the woman. "My name's Marion."

"I'm Elsie, like the cow," Mom joked.

From that moment on, they were friends. My mother's gift for friendship came from her father. My grandfather artfully employed a firm handshake, a youthful smile, and a self-effacing joke to turn strangers into friends.

After some small talk, Mom turned and shouted between the houses and toward the lane, "Pudgie! Come here a minute?"

Big Lou had given me that nickname when I was an infant.

I hated it.

I came running to my mother. She lifted me over the picket fence.

Marion called, "Michael!"

Her little blonde-haired son dropped his metal sand pail and ran to his mother.

"This little boy might be your new friend," she whispered to him as she gently lifted him and held him on her hip.

Mike and I looked at each other, then turned away, and went back to what we were doing.

Our mothers just rolled their eyes.

Soon Marion returned to hanging her laundry, and my mother wandered back toward the front of the house.

Reaching the front lawn, she absorbed the atmosphere of Glen Lane. Beth and I played like puppies on the double sidewalk. The flagpole of Park Elementary School less than a block away towered over the garages at the end of the lane. The blossoming sour cherry tree, the garden space, and the gleaming white picket fence in the backyard must have formed a permanent Kodachrome snapshot in her mind.

Big Lou and the agent had emerged from the house and stood on the front porch. My father with his familiar scowl smoked a cigarette. The agent, also scowling, waited for my mother to return so he could move on to another customer and, perhaps, a sale.

Mom walked with her arms folded and her head down toward the two men. She stopped in front of them, lifted her head, and said, "We'll take it."

Chapter 2

Following my mother's statement, Big Lou's mouth dropped open. His cigarette fell from his lips and tiny glowing embers of tobacco bounced on the concrete porch steps like a miniature fireworks display…we had found a home.

Over the next three years, Mike and I formed a friendship.

"My name's 'Sergeant Friday' today," Mike said.

"You were 'Friday' yesterday!" I protested.

"Yeah, but you were him two times before!"

"Okay, but I'm 'Sergeant Friday' tomorrow."

It never mattered who was 'Sergeant Friday.' Our favorite television-police-name always surfaced.

"Do you see what I see, Joe?'

"Looks like a body in the Charlestons' bushes, Joe!"

"Let's go take a look, Joe."

"Okay, Joe!"

On the morning of June 1st, 1956, Mike and I played *Dragnet* on Mike's front lawn. Our mothers drank coffee and gossiped inside his house. I was five-years-old, and Mike was four. He had short stiff blond hair and big blue-green eyes that widened and glared whenever anger overwhelmed him. Anger forced him to breathe like an asthmatic between his teeth while his fists clenched and unclenched uncontrollably. Happiness produced an immediate contagious giggle that often forced him to double over onto the ground and hyperventilate. Although a full year younger than I, his size, strength, quickness, and mentality equaled mine throughout our childhood.

We were alike in ways that bonded us like brothers. We both loved the action TV shows: *Dragnet, Roy Rogers, Gene Autry, M-Squad,* and *Have Gun Will Travel.* Our joy of reenacting the roles of heroic and villainous characters from our favorite episodes bonded us further.

Just as in the real TV drama, we carefully approached the Charlestons' front lawn directly across the double sidewalk in front of Mike's front lawn. We peeked over the bushes like miniature TV cops viewing a dead body.

Mr. Charleston, looking like Boris Karloff's Frankenstein and holding a stepstool and a paper bag, appeared on his front porch. He was a burly-looking man in his fifties with thinning gray hair and a big beer gut that forced his torn sleeveless T-shirt out of his work pants and exposed his hairy navel. At first, he looked straight ahead and didn't see us at all. Then, he glanced to his right, spotted us and bellowed, "How many times I gotta' tell you kids ta' stay off my lawn! Go play on your own Goddamn lawns!"

We darted toward Mike's lawn, but an adult screaming at kids was so common back then, he hadn't scared us much. From the safety of Mike's property, we watched him.

Mr. Charleston took his stepstool and placed it below a window on the face of his house, not far from where the bushes hid our corpse. From the paper bag he took a squeegee and squirt bottle full of blue fluid. He climbed the stepstool and placed himself directly in front of the window.

With his back turned to us he presented a perfect opportunity for two little boys to act like two little boys, so we made monster-like faces at him and rude noises that we hoped he couldn't hear. He continued his work; either he didn't hear us, or he was ignoring us.

Then, as if pushed by an alien force, Mr. Charleston fell backwards from his stepstool, landed on his bushes, and rolled onto the ground. Mike and I were connoisseurs of *The Three Stooges*, and this stunt rivaled any slapstick we'd seen, and we burst into laughter.

But Mr. Charleston was holding his chest and gasping for air.

We stopped laughing, and Mike ran into his house and called for his mother. From his front lawn, Mr. Charleston turned and looked at me with helpless, painful fear in his eyes. I wanted to run, but I couldn't. Fear and shame shot through me.

I had mocked and laughed at him, and now he might be dying.

Mrs. Charleston, a heavy-set woman, ran from her house and cradled her husband. My mother and Mike's mother came running

Someone had called an ambulance, and the distant siren grew louder and louder. Neighbors trying to comfort Mr. and Mrs. Charleston filled the double sidewalk. The ambulance drove right up the lane to where Mr. Charleston lay. The attendants turned him over and rested him on the stretcher, and it was evident to everyone that he was dead. Our mothers walked Mrs. Charleston to the ambulance and helped her into the back to ride with her husband.

Neighbors stood around after the ambulance sped away and said useless things such as, "I just saw him last night, and he was fine!"

"Geez, and he was just getting ready to retire."

"What's she gonna' do now?"

"Goes to show ya', ya' never know. Ya' just never know."

After a short time, the crowd dispersed. I found myself alone on the lawn, just as I had been when Mr. Charleston looked at me with those fearful eyes.

As I started to walk home I heard the familiar tinkling bells of the Good Humor truck coming down LaSalle Street.

Kids ran to buy Popsicles and ice cream as if nothing had happened.

I listened briefly to the tolling little bells and the laughter of the kids, and then I ran to join the others.

Chapter 3

The summer started with Mr. Charleston's death and ended with my first day of school. On that first day, my mother walked me to Park Elementary School, less than a block from our house. Beth left early to avoid the embarrassment of being seen walking to school with her mother. Mike waved from his kitchen window as we left.

Actually, he was more excited about me starting school than I was. Mike was an only child at the time. His parents convinced him that school was fun and exciting, so he was eager to experience that fun and excitement vicariously through me.

The image that I recall after that is a line of little kids bawling and clutching their moms who were bawling and clutching their kids.

After the painful mother-child separations, Miss Hickey, the kindergarten teacher, took guardianship of us. Being taught by Miss Hickey was a rite of passage that every kid in my neighborhood had to experience. An elderly and tyrannical spinster schoolteacher, she wore winged black-rimmed glasses and combed her short black-dyed hair straight back. As if to remind others or herself that she commanded the respect that comes with age, she left a single-inch column of her hair its natural gray-ash color; it ran from the top of her forehead and tapered to the back of her neck.

"Okay," Miss Hickey began, as everyone sat cross-legged on the warm tile floor and faced her, seated on a wooden chair, "let's get to know each other. We'll start with me; I am Miss Hickey, your teacher, and for the time we spend together, I am your mother, your father, and your God. That's all you need to know about me. Now let's get to know you. Young lady with the pretty blue and white dress, please stand up and tell us your name."

The girl sitting next to me rose to her feet and rocked from one black and white saddle shoe and white anklet sock to the other. Her ruffled dress fluffed out and over my head like an umbrella.

"My name is Susanne,"

"Susanne! What a pretty name!" Miss Hickey exclaimed, "And we will remember Susanne for her long beautiful blonde hair! And how about you, boy?"

I peered from under Susanne's dress.

"Yes, you!" she said like a drill sergeant. "Stand up and tell us your name!"

I stood up. My nervousness took a different form from Susanne's. My body stood like a soldier at attention. I spoke as if I were in boot camp. "My name is Louis, ma'am!"

"Louis! Well, we'll remember Louis from those thick yellow-rimmed glasses that he's wearing!"

Everyone broke into laughter.

Time may have distorted the events of that day, but, that shocking embarrassing moment scorched my memory forever. It was something like "that feeling" when Mr. Charleston looked at me before he died... but a little different, too. I didn't feel vulnerable like when I faced death; I felt aggressive. I didn't know what to do...so I laughed with them and sat down.

A new feeling evolved called self-consciousness. Louis evolved—a "pudgie" little boy with curly brown hair; he wore thick glasses to correct what the doctor called "lazy eye," which meant that the left eye crossed inward and made him look like a freak without his glasses This humiliated and hostile little man vowed revenge on Miss Hickey as he secretly rubbed a booger into Susanne's pretty blue and white dress.

Chapter 4

I raced to the pedal car and jumped into the seat. I turned around, looked back (just as I had seen Big Lou do), and pedaled backward to a safe area. Just as I turned to pedal forward a strange sensation hit me. Perhaps Miss Hickey should have mentioned the rule: *Do not urinate in the pedal cars*. The warm urine, previously on the metal pedal car seat, had now seeped through my corduroy pants, my Superman underwear and onto my ass.

Oh God, what was I going to do? I walked to Miss Hickey's desk. In a whisper I tried not to interrupt her introspection. "Miss Hickey, someone peed in the pedal car and now it's on my pants."

She blew a smoke ring and stared at me a moment. "You peed in your pants? Oh my God! They don't pay me enough!"

"No, see—"

She grabbed me by the collar and marched me to the front office.

"Wait here!" she barked and left me standing in the hallway. She said something to the secretary, and I heard the secretary laugh.

Miss Hickey left the office, walked past me, said, "Just wait here," and went back to the room.

Within minutes my mother was there to walk me home.

Every day seemed to get worse. We sat on the warm tile while she sat at the piano which forced us to endure the sight of her bony, hairy varicose legs. Then, instead of teaching us an inspiring or fun song, she taught us to sing "Go Tell Aunt Rody, the Old Gray Goose is Dead."

On the first day Miss Hickey had told the class to bring a small clean rug with our name taped to it. In the afternoon for twenty minutes or so each child lay on his or her rug and tried to sleep. About a minute into our first nap time Craig whispered loud enough for every kid to hear, "Hey, listen to this…" then made a farting noise. Everyone giggled and more improvised noises followed. Miss Hickey was the only one napping at her desk.

I hated school, I hated Miss Hickey and I hated myself; my recollections are clear on that. Perhaps this hatred matured me because another selfless hate haunted me: breaking the truth about school to my surrogate brother, Mike.

* * *

Sunday, 5:10 a.m.

Beth, Wayne, Dorinda, and I sit silently on the stiff vinyl furniture in the "family" waiting room of the hospital's Intensive Care Unit. The "family" waiting room, small and windowless, contains a box of Kleenex, a wall telephone, and no magazines.

We had just visited or perhaps viewed my mother in her room. Machines, tubes, and electronic monitors kept her peaceful body alive. A beeping green dot leaving an arcing trail across a screen reflects the beating of her heart.

A chunky middle-aged nurse appears in the doorway and mechanically recites, "I know this is hard on all of you, but you need to make a decision about continuing the life support. I know what I'd do if it was my mother."

"Well, it's not your mother," I return, "and we're waiting for our younger sister."

Nurse "Ratchet," as we had nicknamed her, turns on the squeaky heels of her white sneakers and leaves. She seems neither affected nor offended by my words.

Moments later, Terri and her teenage daughters stand in the doorway. Bob must be parking the car. Her eyes, nose, and mouth wrinkle toward the center of her face. She will burst into tears as soon as she hears the truth about our mom…so I lie, "Everything's gonna' be okay."

* * *

"Give?"

"No!"

"Give now?"

"No!"

Mike wrestled my shoulders back to the ground and pinned them down with all his weight against his palms as I squirmed to break loose and get to my feet. That's how kids our age fought back then…no punches, no kicks, just wrestling until one kid yelled, "I give!" and conceded the loss.

Mike negotiated, "Tell me about school, and I'll let you up!"

After struggling for some time, I pleaded, "Okay, Okay, I give! Let me up!"

He let me up.

He was wide-eyed and intense. I had never seen him so anxious to hear me speak. I sensed his passion and excitement for school, and I didn't want to give him the story of my humiliating experience in kindergarten and my hatred for Miss Hickey. "School is…not really school." I didn't know what to say. We had been wrestling on the cool thick grass on our front lawn. Beth watched *The Howdy Doody Show* on our black-and-white TV, and the beeping of *Clarabelle the Clown*'s signature horn squeaked from the TV's speaker through our screen door. "It's really a place called Clown Town!"

"Clown Town?"

"Yeah, Clown Town. You go there and there are clowns everywhere. Every kid has his own clown, and the clown is 'sposed to keep you happy all day!"

"No!"

"Yeah."

"Yeah?"

"Yeah."

"What's your clown's name?"

"His name?" I scanned the front lawn. My Chicago Cubs baseball cap lay on the grass as a result of our wrestling match. "Cubbie!"

"Cubbie? Cool! So, what's he do? What happens?"

"Ya' know those cool lookin' hot rods the teenagers sometimes drive down LaSalle Street?"

"Yeah?"

"Well, Cubbie took me outside the school, and there, on the curb, in the circle part in front of the school…"

"Yeah?"

"All the teenagers with their hot rods were there!"

"No!"

"Yeah, and Cubbie says, 'Which one ya' wanta' ride in, Lou?' He calls me, Lou, not Pudgie, and I point to the blue one with the fire painted on it and the shiny metal stuff on the motor. He takes me to the car, the teenager says, 'Hop in, man!' So, I jump in the front seat, and the teenager takes me for a real fast ride around that circle until it's time to go home!"

"Wow! Wow! Wow!" Mike said as if he had been on the ride, too.

I had found a way out for the moment.

Every day Mike challenged my imagination, and every day I met the challenge. On Wednesday, Roy Rogers, Dale Evans, and Trigger (our favorite TV cowboy characters) came to school. The next day Cubbie brought Ernie Banks, the new slugger for the Chicago Cubs, and he showed me how to play baseball.

On my short walk home from school on Friday I must have felt slightly relieved. Mike had taken the train to downtown Chicago with his mother; I wouldn't be pressed to make up a Clown Town story. Actually, I was probably a little disappointed, also. I rather enjoyed making up stories.

What had I really learned after completing my first week of school? Contemplating this question, I picked up a rock and blindly threw it at the street lamp on the corner of 142nd and Wentworth. The rock hit the bulb, and a tinkling sound of shattered glass rang out. No one witnessed this except me, and I wasn't going to tell anyone.

Chapter 5

My bed rocked as if the wake of a speedboat traveled beneath my mattress.

"Wake up, Pudge, Uncle's here. He's stayin' at my house. Ya' gotta' meet 'im!"

My bleary eyes gradually focused on Mike's eager face while my head still rested on my soft pillow. Oh yeah, I thought, it's Saturday; Mike was downtown with his mom after I returned from school. No Clown Town story. Now I had to come up with something first thing in the morning! But Mike didn't even mention Clown Town.

"C'mon, he's havin' breakfast now. He's cool. Ya' gotta meet 'im!"

"Okay! Okay!"

I dressed and followed Mike downstairs. My mother had a bowl of Cheerios and a glass of milk waiting for me on the kitchen table. Big Lou had left for work at the Acme Steel mill, and Beth had already eaten and was out playing with her friends. Terri, my younger sister less than a year-old, sat in her high chair and futilely tried to find her mouth with a handful of brown gelatin-like baby food.

"Sit down and eat your breakfast," Mom ordered, as she flitted around the kitchen cleaning up. "Michael was pounding on the door early this morning wanting you to meet his uncle, and it was about time you got up, so I sent him upstairs to wake you. Michael, can I fix you something?"

"No, thanks, Elsie." (Yes, we called each other's parents by their first name.) "Soon as Pudge finishes, I'm havin' breakfast with Uncle!"

I forced my breakfast down, and we headed out the back door and across the alley to Mike's house. He and his mother had taken the train downtown to meet his uncle at the Greyhound Bus Terminal on Randolph Street on Friday. His uncle's real name was Jim, but everyone called him 'J.P.' He had just finished college in Mississippi, and he would be staying with Mike, Marion, Mickey (Mike's dad), and Grandma Hale (Marion's mother) until he landed a good job.

The backdoor of Mike's house opened right to the kitchen/dinette area, so as soon as we walked inside I saw J.P. He sat at the small round kitchen table, wore a plain white T-shirt, blue jeans rolled up at the cuffs, white socks, and penny loafers, and held a cigarette in one hand and a cup of coffee in the other. He was a small, thin, but handsome young man with prematurely thinning brown hair. He rested his cigarette in a glass ashtray on the table, lazily reached over, and extended his hand. "You must be Pudge," he said in a slight southern drawl.

"Yeah," I answered and shook his hand.

"You can just call me J.P.," he instructed. Mike beamed proudly as he stared at his uncle. Grandma Hale, J.P.'s mother, sat at the table and beamed at her son, also. She was a very feeble, thin old woman; however, she often cooked, gardened, and performed household chores at her own slow but deliberate pace.

J.P. was the pride of the family, not just because he was the first in the family to graduate from college with a Master's degree, but he was also something of a musical genius; he could pick up any type of musical instrument and instinctively play it. His specialty was percussion.

Mickey, Mike's father, breezed into the kitchen and kissed Marion on the forehead as he adjusted his suit coat over his shoulders. He was a tall handsome man with wavy black hair who always carried a sense of confidence and purpose with him. As the manager of several White Castle hamburger restaurants on Chicago's southside, he worked many hours throughout the week.

"Good mornin', Momma." He respectfully acknowledged Grandma Hale, then to rest of us, "Hey, men."

We returned "good mornings."

"Gotta' run, guys." He dropped a set of keys on the table in front of J.P. "I'll take Marion's car. J.P., if you need to go somewhere you can use mine." He hurried out the front door.

"Thanks, Mick!" J.P. yelled after him.

"You guys got anything important to do today?" J.P. asked us as he sipped his coffee.

Saturday, a no-school day, meant for kids our age that we had everything and nothing to do. Mike asked him what he was doing.

"I need to go downtown and buy some interviewing clothes. Thought maybe you guys might want to come along," J.P. said as he stretched his arms.

The mystery and the adventure of the unknown always attracted Mike and me, so we eagerly agreed to go.

J.P. drove Mickey's all white 1956 Chrysler down the ramp of the underground parking garage on Michigan Avenue. After parking, we emerged from a stairwell to Michigan Avenue and Randolph Street, the heart of downtown Chicago's Loop. I had never been downtown. Mike, however, had been to the Loop many times, because his mother worked in the lost and found department of the Illinois Central Railroad, the commuter train running from the south suburbs to downtown.

The sounds of the big city frightened me. The heavy steel wheels of the elevated train against the rusted tracks clacked above us. Horns quacked from the cars, distant sirens faded in and out, and a jackhammer rhythmically beat against a crumbling concrete sidewalk.

We walked westward on Randolph toward State Street, but before reaching State we stopped by the flashing lights of a brightly lit storefront. A neon genie beckoned for people to come in and have fun.

J.P. pulled out four single dollar bills and gave us each two.

"Okay, guys, here's the deal: Go in there and spend this money, but don't leave the place until I get back."

He opened the door and made sure we were safely off the street, then disappeared. It was like a kid's dream inside: pinball machines, skittle ball games, carnival prizes for ring toss, penny arcade machines, photo machines, and trinkets for sale. It was a carnival without the rides. The constant carnival music and flashing lights made us feel as if we were inside a giant jukebox.

The next hour seemed to disappear as we raced from one attraction to the other. As we prepared to put more coins into a pinball machine, we noticed J.P. standing at the front entrance. He had a Marshall Field's shopping bag in each hand, so he motioned with his head for us to come over to him. We left the pinball machine and sauntered toward him.

"You guys had about enough?" he asked

We showed him that we each had about a dollar left.

"Well, I guess we'll have to do something about that."

We followed him back to the underground parking garage, down the stairwell and into the car.

It was 1956; the Dan Ryan Expressway hadn't been built yet, so people from the southside or south suburbs who traveled to and from downtown Chicago ultimately had to use Lake Shore Drive. The "Drive" provided the scenic views of Lake Michigan and a regatta of boats from the windows on one side of the car and the Chicago skyline from the other. Lake Shore Drive ended on 95th and Stoney Island Avenue, the same location as Play Land, a children's amusement park.

J.P parked the Chrysler in the gravel parking lot and gave us these instructions, "Go on in and spend the rest of your money. Then come over to that beer stand where I'll be waiting and try not to take too long; it's too early in the day for me to get tanked."

Mike and I could hardly believe our good fortune; we raced into the park and purchased tickets for the roller coaster. A tall wooden electrical pole with colorful advertising flyers stapled to it diverted my attention while we stood in the long line to board the ride. One flyer was a collage of clowns, balloons, and circus animals with bold lettered words above it. I was too young to read the words, but in retrospect it was probably an ad for the Shrine Circus that came to Chicago every fall during the 1950s and 60s.

My hands began to sweat, and my stomach felt queasy. It wasn't fear of the rollercoaster ride; I worried about Mike's disappointment when eventually he'd learn the truth about Clown Town.

Chapter 6

"So, how was school?" Big Lou began supper with his ritualistic question.

"It was okay." Beth shrugged with her ritualistic answer as she stared at her plate and made tracks in her mashed potatoes with her fork.

"Well," I began. Now that I was in school, I felt that I should be a part of this ritual. "This kid, Craig, got mad and socked this girl, Brenda, in the stomach, so Miss Hickey—"

"Sit up like a lady!" my father interrupted as he corrected Beth's posture.

After a short pause, my mother nodded, indicating for me to continue.

"So Miss Hickey grabbed Craig, and—"

"Don't talk with your mouth full of food!" he interrupted again. "My God! Do you have to eat like a pig?"

That was my father's standard reaction to me; he either ignored me or corrected me. My conclusion: He hated me. Big Lou was a perfectionist. When he saw imperfection, he either ignored it or tried to make it perfect. He must have seen me, this little pudgy boy with a turned-in left eye, as his own imperfect creation. His first reaction was to make his creation perfect. He'd had my mother take me to an eye specialist, Dr. Daley. The doctor put glasses on me and told my mother that in time the glasses would correct my "lazy" left eye. In the interim, I walked around with thick yellow-rimmed glasses that reminded my dad of imperfection. So he tried to ignore me.

That night, however, he reacted in an unexpected way.

After supper, the whole family sat in front of the TV set. This was Monday night, *Lucy* night. Specifically, it was October 8th, 1956, and the *I Love Lucy Show* aired an episode titled "Little Ricky Plays the Drums." In this episode a five-year-old actor showed his prodigious talent of playing the drums.

From my little "TV stool" I watched the young actor and was mesmerized. I mimicked Little Ricky's every move-ment and facial expression as he played the drums.

Big Lou roared with laughter and encouraged me, "That's it! That's it! You've got it!"

"Hey, Dad, look at me!" I said in the days that fol-lowed, and I would play my invisible drums with my invisible drumsticks. Then I looked for his approving smile.

Months later, on Christmas day, I ripped off the wrap-ping paper thinly disguising the toy drum set. It really wasn't much—a miniature metal base drum with a foot pedal, two little tom-tom drums and an attached cymbal. The sticks were short thick pieces of rounded wood with plastic beads attached to the tapered ends. My parents knew that they had made a mistake as soon as I began playing as if I were Little Ricky. The obvious differences were that Little Ricky had talent, and the sound of drums could be controlled with a TV set volume dial. Nevertheless, my family endured my drum solos in exchange for seeing my happiness.

Big Lou received an Eastman Kodak 8-millimeter movie camera that Christmas day with all the attachments and was as obsessed with his new toy as I with mine. He busied himself piecing it together and figuring out how to use it. He couldn't put it down.

He spent a great deal of footage shooting me playing the drums.

The day after Christmas, the joy of seeing and hearing me play the drums wore off. My toy drums and I were banished upstairs to my room where my playing could still be heard but at a much more pleasant-sounding distance. My parents must have thought that my enthusiasm for the drums would be the same as that for all my toys; I would lose interest in a few weeks and move on to something else.

They were wrong. After three weeks I was still banging away.

"It's done," my father announced after work. "My first movie film! I just picked it up at the drugstore. Let's take a look at it."

"Are you forgetting something?" Mom said as she peeled carrots in the sink.

Big Lou immediately felt stupid for his oversight, but then blurted, "Call Pa. He's got a projector and screen!"

"Pa" was my grandfather, my mother's father. He was a gregarious man with a positive attitude, quite the opposite of Big Lou. Dad's temporary enthusiasm for home movies, however, provided a bond between them. Grandpa loved gadgetry and had been a home movie buff from its outset in the early 1950s. He bought a new Ford every two years because

Fords fulfilled his need for gadgetry (a convertible hardtop that mechanically disappeared into the trunk, etc.), and Fords always seemed to be smiling, just like him. Big Lou, on the other hand, drove an unpopular, dour looking, black and red 1953 Nash.

After dinner we drove to my grandparents' home in the near south suburb of Harvey. Grandpa already had the movie projector and screen set up in the living room. My grandmother, who possessed the same positive qualities of my grandfather, worked preparing a meal in her kitchen for us. No amount of arguing could convince her that we had already eaten, and we were not hungry. To her, anyone who entered her house was underfed, and she provided the remedy.

We sat in silence in the darkened living room and stared at the barely visible movie screen on its tripod in front of us. Suddenly, the click of the projector switch produced a large white rectangle of light from the tiny bulb of the projector onto the movie screen. The clickety-click of the film as it passed through the projector gears and by the bulb produced spotted images from the leader tape onto the screen....and shortly after....Christmas morning appeared again!

"Ooooh! Look at the tree and the lights!"

"How come it's so wobbly?" I asked.

"Because that contraption Dad was aiming around weighs about a thousand pounds," Beth said.

Big Lou gave us a nasty look.

"There we all are," Mom narrated, "waving at the camera and talking to it, as if there was sound."

"How come we're all squintin' and shadin' our eyes?" I asked.

"Because lookin' at that contraption was like starin' into the sun," Beth answered.

"That's enough, young lady," my father warned.

"Oh," my grandmother remarked sympathetically, "see how much Pudgie likes beating on those drums."

"Oh, my God! Lou!" Mom gasped, then broke into laughter with everyone else.

All that time I had thought my father was patiently recording my drum solos; he was actually practicing the use of the camera's zoom lens. Specifically, he zoomed in and out on the open fly of my pajama bottoms. The film verified two facts: one, I really enjoyed playing the drums, and two, I was a male.

Chapter 7

"What is it?" I asked, although I was tempted to use Big Lou's vernacular and ask, "What the hell is it?"

"It's a practice pad," my mother said.

"What d'ya' practice doin', killin' bugs?"

It was a foot-square flat piece of finished wood with a half-inch-thick piece of round black rubber about the size of a coffee cup saucer sunk into the center of it.

"No, smart ass," my father answered as if any idiot could figure out its purpose. "It's to practice your Gene Krupa moves without the Goddamn noise!"

Mom shot Big Lou a look of annoyance and added, "And these are real drumsticks that J.P. picked out for you. He also agreed to give you some lessons."

The six weeks between Christmas and this day, my birthday, passed routinely: Miss Hickey continued to yell and to humiliate me; occasionally, Mike forced me to make up more Clown Town stories; and I banged away on my toy drum set in my upstairs bedroom. J.P. had found a job working downtown, but he wasn't happy. The job had nothing to do with music, and he became just another commuter to downtown Chicago. To supplement his income and probably his state of mind, he gave private music lessons on Saturdays and a few nights after work. The lessons took place at Mike's house where J.P. took residence.

"First thing you're going to learn is how to sit," he said.

"What?"

"That's right. Sit on the stool."

I rolled my eyes and plopped down on the swivel stool and sort of shifted from side to side.

"Wrong. Stand up and try it again," he said.

I thought he was kidding; I just laughed.

He physically stood me up, sat me down, and said, "Sit down, feet forward, heels flat, back straight and relaxed... That's it...No, now you're slouching, sit up...relax...knees apart...not that far apart...you're slouching again...good..."

I spent most of my first lesson learning how to sit. When he was finally satisfied that I could sit properly, he brought out an old dulling nickel-plated snare drum on a stand from the closet and adjusted the stand to the correct height. I finally thought, here we go!

He placed the snare and stand between my knees, but as I leaned forward he pulled it back. We kept this pantomime going until I realized that when I stopped slouching, the drum stayed.

J.P. sat back, looked at me, smiled and said, "You look good! That's it. Come back next Saturday. In the meantime, practice sitting in front of your practice pad."

I was stunned…but obedient. Every night I practiced sitting in front of my practice pad and visualized J.P. snagging the pad away if I leaned forward.

At the next lesson, J.P. examined my posture and rewarded me with the snare drum between my knees; he smiled when he noticed that I didn't slouch forward.

"Well, I guess you're ready to use your sticks," he said as he took them from my hands. He demonstrated as he spoke. "Hold your left hand, palm up, over the drum like this, and your right hand, palm down, like this."

When he was satisfied with the positioning of my hands, he put a stick in each and carefully curled my fingers around them. He positioned the bead ends over the drum precisely, then sat back and examined his product. With his hand on his chin and a slight frown on his face, he remarked, "Not bad, not bad. Now turn your palm down, and I want you to strike the drum with the left stick, but use only your wrist."

I struck the drum head, something I had been waiting to do for a week.

"No! No!" he said in a serious yet patient tone. "Don't use your hand…Don't use your arm…Use your wrist…once again…better…much better!"

We did the same with the right stick. Right. Left. Right. Left. Right. Right. Left. Left. Repeat.

That was lesson number two.

I practiced every night that week in my room with my practice pad. Sometimes I wasn't sure whether I was taking drum lessons or going through some kind of slow physical therapy.

On the third lesson he checked to see if I had practiced. When he was satisfied, he held up two books. "This
one's called *How to Read Music*, and this one's called *The 26
Drum Rudiments*. When we finish both books, you'll be a
drummer—how good a drummer will depend on you and
how much you practice."

Every week I learned a little more about drumming
and reading music. Between lessons I practiced striking the
practice pad and counting aloud, "Quarter notes: 1-2-3-4;
Eighth notes: 1-and-2-and-3-and-4-and; Sixteenth notes: 1-e-
and-a-2-e-and-a-3-e-and-a-4-e-and-a."

After some time, I'd stop and wonder what J.P. would
say. That's when I'd hear Beth and her friends in her room
next to mine as they mimicked, "1-e-and-a-2-e-and-a…"

"Shut up!"

They'd just laugh, and I'd start up again but try to
count more quietly. Whenever I'd stop, they'd start in again,
"1-e-and-a-2-e-and-a-3-e-and-a…Ma-a, he's hittin' us with
those stupid drumsticks again!"

When I arrived at Mike's back door for another lesson, I was surprised to see only Marion and Grandma Hale
sitting at the dinette table and drinking coffee.

"They're all in the back room for some reason,
honey," Marion said. "Go on back there."

Mike, wearing his Davy Crockett pajamas, sat on the
couch, and watched the *Mighty Mouse* cartoon show.
Mickey, in his dress paints and smoking jacket, sat in his
maroon leather lounge chair. Both wore smiles of mischievous children .

"Sit down, Pudge," Mickey instructed. "He'll be
down pretty soon. You came just in time for the show."

I sat in the rocker and watched *Mighty Mouse* with Mike.

After a few minutes, J.P. came down dressed in his usual Saturday attire—white T-shirt, jeans, penny loafers.

"Mornin', boys," he greeted us as he grabbed his pack of Winstons from the end table next to Mickey. "Damn," he said as he stared into the pack, "I thought I had more than just one left. Guess I better cut down."

He pulled a silver-plated lighter from his pocket and lit the cigarette now held firmly between his lips. Before he could enjoy his first morning drag, however, POW! The cigarette blew up and J.P. had tiny specs of brown tobacco all over his face.

"What the hell!" he shrieked although a smile was already starting to form on his face; he sensed that he was a victim of one of Mickey's practical jokes.

Mike and Mickey roared, and I joined them even though I wasn't fully aware of what was going on.

Marion ran into the back room and scolded, "What was that? What are you little boys—referring to all of us—up to now?"

"They're called cigarette loads," Mickey confessed and produced a small white paper packet from his smoking jacket pocket. The top of the packet was already torn open, and he spilled a few loads onto the end table to show us. They looked like tiny rectangles of thin brown poster board. "A guy at the Roseland White Castle gave them to me. You just put one in the end of a cigarette, and when someone lights it—POW! They got me good with it yesterday."

"Well, you scared the hell outa' me," J.P. admitted.

We all laughed again.

"All right," Mickey said, "Let's let these musicians get to work." He led everyone out the room, except J.P. and me.

"Whew! Well, I think I've got my senses back," J.P. sighed, took a cigarette from the pack Mickey had left, carefully examined it, lit it and took a long drag. "Let's get to work."

He brought out the snare, and it was business as usual.

* * *

Sunday, 5:45 a.m.

"When I disengage the life support system, she'll remain unconscious. She won't feel a thing," Nurse "Ratchet" tutors us.

Beth and Terri hover on each side of my mother's bed. Each clasps one of her hands as the nurse manipulates the controls of the system. I stand at the foot of the bed while Wayne, Bob, Dorinda, and my nieces hold hands off to the side.

The nurse steps back, and the beeping green dot slowly flattens out its wave-like journey across the monitor screen. Just before it flattens, Mom's eyes open wide.

"She's squeezing my hand!" Terri says through her tears. "She said she wouldn't feel a thing, but she's squeezing my hand!"

Beth can't speak, but she acknowledges with nods that Mom squeezes her hand, also.

Mom stares blankly into nowhere…or somewhere. Her grip loosens from my sisters' hands.

Nurse "Ratchet" gently moves Beth aside, wipes blood from the corners of Mom's mouth with tissue, and closes her eyelids.

"It's over," she says.

We hug each other. Not knowing exactly what to do, we file back to the "family" room. A young nurse approaches me and says, "I'm sorry, but there are some forms to sign now."

I mechanically follow her to the center nurses' station. She places a small stack of papers on the counter. She explains the purpose of the first sheet, but I'm not listening. Behind her is the open door to the nurses' break room. Nurse "Ratchet" is standing inside the doorway, smoking, and listening to someone out of my sight. She tilts her head back, blows smoke at the ceiling, and laughs at something the other person has said.

I hate her.

* * *

"All right, let's form our girls' line and boys' line for milk time!" Miss Hickey yelled over the happy children's voices during play time.

Like soldiers at the end of basic training, they obediently formed lines and marched toward the milk crates in response to "Sergeant" Hickey's command. After eight months of kindergarten, the children had acquired a taste for the souring milk through the cheap paper straws, and they routinely sat at the long wooden tables and worked the waxy paper caps from the milk bottles.

POW! SPLASH! "Ahhhhh!"

Every child forgot his or her nasty-tasting milk and looked up. Miss Hickey looked like a cartoon character with a shredded cigarette between her lips, bits of tobacco on her glasses and cheeks, and spilled coffee soaking her desk blotter and dripping onto her dress.

"What the h—," she stopped herself from cursing and then ran to the teachers' lounge to clean up.

When I sucked the creamy fluid through the straw, it didn't weaken and flatten as usual; it stayed strong, and the milk tasted unusually sweet that day.

Chapter 8

"Okay, who wants to start show-and-tell today? Gregory? Good stand up dear…" Miss Hickey acted as if a cigarette had never exploded in her face the day before.

A primal anger swelled within me as I sat listening to show-and-tell. Gregory showed his store-bought rock collection, and I reached into the puzzle shelf and extracted a small wooden puzzle piece. I quickly wound up and hurled the piece at Gregory, hitting him squarely in the chest. I didn't know why I did it; I just did it.

Some kids laughed, which I appreciated, but most of them stared with astonishment at me. Miss Hickey dismissed my action and me, as usual.

"Louis! What are you doing!" It was more of a yell than a question. "Get over in that chair, face the wall, and stay there the rest of the day!"

That was it…no further punishment…no call home. Since this was the end of the school year, maybe Miss Hickey didn't want to be bothered with parent conferences and disciplinary paperwork; however, my final report card, which had numerous 'S's and 'U's for Satisfactory and Unsatisfactory, included a closing comment:

Louis has a very bad temper for a boy of his age.

After the final day of school, I brought the report card home and gave it to my mother. She congratulated me on my 'S's, asked about my 'U's, and frowned at the comment. She said nothing and simply put the report card in the kitchen drawer.

I dreaded supper that evening. My report card would surely be a hot topic. Big Lou retired his ritualistic question, "How was school today?" for the summer, but during dinner he took the report card from the drawer and asked me, "What does this mean?"

"What?" I said.

"The comment."

"I don't know. I can't read yet."

"Don't get smart!"

Obviously, my father didn't see the humor in my response, but Beth did. She giggled, and Big Lou looked at her as if she had cursed. Then he read from the report card, "Louis has a very bad temper for a boy of his age."

I thought for a moment. No answer came to me except, "I guess I'm not old enough to get pissed off."

He stood up, disregarding the glassware, plates, and food, and backhanded me across my cheek.

The discussion was over.

"Sit down, Pudge," J.P. said as he put his cigarette out in a thick clear glass ashtray.

He sat at the kitchen table drinking coffee and smoking a cigarette that Saturday morning when I arrived for my lesson; he wasn't smiling.

"This is going to have to be our last lesson. I've been offered a job as the assistant band director at the University of

Florida in Gainesville. It's the chance I've been waiting for, and I'm taking it. I'm leaving next Saturday. Sorry, pal, but I want you to keep practicing until you find another teacher."

I didn't know what to say. I was as happy as a little kid could be for an adult who got his big break—which means I wasn't very happy at all. I was unhappy for myself because I knew this might be my last drum lesson. The lessons were convenient because J.P. lived across the alley, and they were cheap, free, because of my friendship with Mike. Finding a new drum teacher would not be a top priority on my parents' financial list.

During the week that followed, I tried to practice each day, but my enthusiasm waned as Saturday approached. By Friday I had nearly lost all interest in the drums.

The sound of gravel and stones crushed beneath the wheels of a car slowly traveling down the alleyway awakened me at about five o'clock that Saturday morning. J.P. parked his 1956 pink and white Crown Victoria in the alleyway between our houses. He had bought the car shortly after landing his job in Chicago.

I slipped on a T-shirt, jeans, my pair of Ked's tennis shoes and quietly tip-toed out of the house. When I got to the alley, Mickey and Marion were helping J.P. load his trunk with luggage. Grandma Hale stood behind them. Only a haze of light illuminated this early summer morning. I wondered why people talked in whispers during this eerie time of day.

"Pudgie, what are you doing up so early? Mike's still sleeping," Mickey whispered as he lit a cigarette.

"I don't know," I answered in a normal tone. "I guess I just wanted to say good-bye."

"Shhhhhh!" they all warned, then laughed and covered their mouths to muffle the sound.

J.P. squatted down, gave me a hug, and said, "Remember, keep practicing, champ."

He stood up, shook hands with Mickey, and promised to drive carefully. He hugged Marion and Grandma Hale and promised them that he would call when he got to Florida. He climbed into his car.

His red taillights got smaller and smaller. They finally vanished when he turned at the end of the alley and headed south. Marion and Mickey walked through their picket fence gate and toward the backdoor of their house.

I stood motionless for some time.

The morning light brightened the alleyway. The tin lid from our neighbor's garbage can lay next to their fence. A furry animal looking for food sat on the overflowing garbage and busily burrowed his head into the wet trash. At first, I thought it was a squirrel, but as I got closer I recognized the skinny tail, short ears, and ugly head of a rat.

To me it was more than just a rat.

The alley was full of rocks, so I looked around for the perfect stone and found it; it had sharp edges and was big enough to do serious damage, but small enough to be hurled with dangerous velocity. The rock pressed against my curled fingers and palm, and the skin burned as the sharp edges scraped against my tightening grip. All my anger and hate focused on the filthy rodent. I mimicked Warren Spahn (my favorite major league pitcher's slow deliberate wind-up) and hurled the rock straight at the rat's head…but I missed. It sailed about a fist above him, ricocheted off a cyclone fence, and disappeared into the anonymity of the other rocks in the alley.

The rat raised its head as if mildly annoyed and continued eating the rotting vegetables and meat from the garbage can.

Chapter 9

Four weeks later, Mike and I relaxed beneath the shade of an elm tree on the grassy corner of LaSalle and 141st, just a half block from our homes. On this typical sweltering Chicago summer day, we perspired beneath our official Davy Crockett coonskin caps. Earlier that year, Walt Disney had aired a tremendously popular TV mini-series *The Adventures of Davy Crockett*. The popularity of the series prompted the marketing of Davy Crockett air rifles, Davy Crockett T-shirts, Davy Crockett pajamas, and even Davy Crockett underwear; Mike and I had it all including the official Davy Crockett cap made of thick warm raccoon fur with a raccoon tail hanging from the back.

We played a game of our own invention called *Name that Car*. The object was to spot a car far down LaSalle or 141st Street and then name the model/make and year before it got close enough for a clear identification.

"That's a '57 DeSoto!" I announced.

"That's no DeSoto, idiot," Mike shot back. "That's a Studebaker."

"Actually," a voice from behind us corrected, "that's a 1957 dusk rose pink and white T-Bird roadster 312, V8, 4-barrel, porthole model."

An older-looking kid with neatly combed brown hair flashed an I-know-more-about-cars-than-you smile at us. His plaid sport shirt and ironed khaki pants reminded Mike and me that we were little kids in our Davy Crockett attire.

"Who are you?" I asked.

"Name's Dwayne. Live over in that house." He pointed to a small ranch house toward the end of 141st Street.

"What grade ya' goin' inta'?" Mike asked.

"Third."

"So how come I never seen ya' at Park School?" I completed the interrogation.

The '57 T-Bird roadster sped past us.

"Cuz I don't go to Park School. I go to Queen of Apostles; you know, the Catholic school on the other side of 144th Street. Say, you guys like cars?"

We nodded.

"I got almost every make and model car from 1955 to 1957 at my house over there. C'mon, I'll show ya's."

Mike and I followed him and wondered how anyone could fit all those cars into one little ranch house, but he did. Dwayne had practically every American car made between 1955 and 1957 in a model car collection that covered an entire basement wall of shelving. He took us through a tour of each car and its special features.

After about an hour, Mike and I left Dwayne's house and walked home. We had acquired two important things that day: a new friend and an appreciation of the flashy styling of 1950s automobiles.

* * *

Monday, 8:30 a.m.

As I gently pull the huge cloth car cover toward me, the overhead fluorescent light in my garage catches the glossy red finish of my 1957 Chevy Belair. The white light on the deep clear-coat body produces sparkling star-like reflections.

We have an appointment at the funeral home at 9:30 to finalize all the arrangements. While Dorinda gets ready, I decide to visit my prize possession, my restored classic '57 Chevy.

That car always cheers me up, and after the last thirty hours of gloom, I need to smile. I carefully open the driver's side door and sit on the shiny red and black upholstery. The interior has that indescribable new-car-smell.

Like a child pretending to drive his father's car in the garage, I pretend it's later in April when all the winter snow has melted and the cold rains have ended; that's when my Chevy and I cruise the streets on clear, warm spring and summer days and nights.

I restored nearly every inch of this once-pile-of-rust to a handsome showpiece. It intoxicates me with pride—me, a fifty-plus year old high school English teacher.

Mom was proud of me, too.

Maybe I should drive it in the funeral procession on Wednesday!

No.

Driving my '57 Chevy would not appropriately honor Mom.

Someday, I will drive it in honor of Ray.

* * *

The next day I sat on my grandparents' front porch in Harvey and wished that it wasn't Sunday afternoon. Our Sunday afternoon ritual reeked of boredom. The ritual consisted of the women (my mother, grandmother, and aunts) preparing a hot meal on a hot day in a hot kitchen, and the men watching golf on a small black-and-white TV set in a hot living room.

This was a special Sunday ritual. My Aunt Dorothy, my mother's younger sister, had recently gotten engaged, and her fiancé, Ray, was coming to dinner to meet the family.

Big deal, I thought.

A cool breeze carried the fresh pine scent from the front lawn tree to my face—at least it was cooler and fresher than the stale stifling air inside the house. Then a vision appeared. The most beautiful car I had ever seen rolled down Lexington Avenue. It was a two-door, white hard top, bright aqua body, flashing flames on each side, fender-skirted, 283 cubic engine1957 Belair Chevrolet. More importantly, it glided to the curb right in front of my grandparents' house. My future Uncle Ray opened the door and stepped out. With his slicked-back blond hair and shades, he looked just like James Dean. He walked up the porch steps, patted me on the head, and said something like, "Hey, sport."

I followed him into the house where my Aunt Dorothy met him and introduced him to the men in the living room. Like children told to wash up before dinner, they stood, shook his hand, and returned to watching golf. After meeting the women in the kitchen, Ray sat down at the kitchen table rather than joining the men in the living room. My grandfather brought him the customary shot-and-a-beer, which he accepted.

I joined him at the kitchen table.

"What's goin' on, man?" He acknowledged me.

"I don't know. How come you're not in there watchin' golf?"

"I hate golf."

I liked him already.

"What do they call you?" he asked.

"They call me Pudge. My name is Lou, but I only like Jim, my middle name."

He laughed, "Okay, Big Jim," and that became the name he called me.

"What do I call you?"

"What do you call her?" he shot back and pointed toward my aunt.

"Dorothy."

"Then just call me Ray."

My grandfather walked into the kitchen, clapped his hands, and rubbed them together, pantomiming, "What mischief can I get into." When I stopped paying attention to him he playfully smacked me on the back of my head and pointed to my grandmother as the culprit.

"Sam," my grandmother reprimanded, "quit acting like a kid and taste the soup. See if it's done."

My grandfather exaggerated his obedience by saluting her and grabbed a dinner soup spoon. He dipped the spoon into the heating pot of chicken broth, carefully sipped it, and wrinkled his face in disappointment.

"Tastes like the chicken walked through it with its boots on!"

Ray and I roared. Ray laughed like a kid; he just let it out.

Big Lou always said grace before Sunday dinner—ironic because he hadn't been to church since his wedding. The family enjoyed watching Ray get accustomed to using his dinner soup spoon. My grandmother's soup spoons were from the "old country," which meant that the width of the spoon was slightly wider than the widest human mouth.

After dinner, the women cleared the table, and the men went back to watching golf. Ray joined the men this time, and I followed. After about five minutes, Ray gave me a look that said, "Let's get out of here," and we left through the front door.

"What do you think of my car?" Ray asked as we stood on the front porch.

"I love it," I said.

"Then let's go for a ride."

"All right!"

We drove a few blocks away to an abandoned road near a shut-down metal plating factory. Within seconds the 283 engine whined, and the Chevy was doing ninety.

"Yeah!" I screamed.

The stretch of road was less than a quarter mile, so we quickly slowed down and just cruised the streets of Harvey.

"Dorothy and I agreed that we'd either get engaged, or I'd spend the ring money on this car. Well, I went ahead and bought the car and somehow bought the ring, too. I don't know. Just seemed like the time for me to settle down." Then he laughed to himself, "Like that's ever gonna' happen. Anyway, when I was about your age my mom died. Couldn't believe it. I was sittin' on a fence and my uncle came up to me and said, 'Your mom's dead.' I said, 'You're a liar!' I remember that. 'You're a liar!' Then, come to find out my dad's seein' this woman the whole time my mom's dyin', and she becomes my stepmother…ah, what's it all matter now? So, you plannin' on goin' to college?"

He stunned me. No one had ever talked to me like that before…like I was a thinking human being and not just a dumb kid.

"Uh…yeah, I guess so."

"Get an education. Me? I goofed around in school. Never took it seriously. Chased girls. Drove a motorcycle. Look at me now. I work my ass off settin' telephone poles for the phone company. I make good money, but like I say, I'm workin' my ass off. I'd rather be sittin' in the office makin' better money and workin' less, like the educated guys."

We drove back to my grandparents' house where my parents, Beth, and Terri waited on the front porch.

"Where you been?" my dad asked.

"I just took him for a ride," Ray answered.

"Nice meeting you, Ray," Big Lou said coldly and extended his hand.

They shook hands robotically, and we climbed into our '53 Nash and headed home.

I couldn't wait to get home and tell Mike about the '57 Chevy and Ray.

"I'm goin' over to Mike's when we get home," I announced.

"Not until you clean up your room," my father countered. "I was up there yesterday. It's a pigsty."

The phone rang as we walked through the front door. My mother ran to answer it, and my father headed back outside to unwind the garden hose and to sprinkle the front lawn. I grabbed an old rag, wet it, and stormed upstairs to my attic bedroom.

Big Lou was right; my room was always messy, but it wasn't exactly a "pigsty." I picked up the "dust bunnies" in the corners of the floor and threw them out the window. I carelessly dusted the desk and a few bookshelves with the wet rag, and simultaneously threw socks, underwear, and various garments into the closet. After shabbily making my bed, I threw the wet rag onto the floor where it miraculously became a mop with my foot and leg operating as the handle. I closed the closet door and *Voila*—a somewhat clean room. I ran downstairs. My mother had just hung up the phone.

"My room's clean. I'm goin' to Mike's," I said.

"Not right now you're not," Mom answered. Her forehead and nose wrinkled into a frown. "Your grandfather just died."

Chapter 10

"Your grandfather's dead," my mother repeated.

My head shook in disbelief. He couldn't be dead, I thought, I just saw him! I backed up slowly and prepared to run to my room.

My mother sensed her mistake and clarified, "Not Grandpa Steffek. Your father's father died."

Without thinking I sighed, "Whew! Thank God!"

My mother put her finger to her lips signifying that I should lower my voice; then, she stepped forward as her face contorted into a frown, slapped me across my face, and whispered, "What an awful thing to say! I hope your father didn't hear you!"

Guilt replaced my feeling of relief. It wasn't that I didn't like my father's father; I hardly knew him. He lived in Hazel Crest, a nearby suburb, with my Aunt Angie. He was an older version of my father: short, stocky, strong, and stoic. My father's characteristic expression was a sulking somber look. His father constantly displayed a shy thin smile. Although he rarely spoke, his thick, hoarse, raspy Italian accent always commanded attention. Years later when I first

saw *The Godfather*, Marlon Brando's Don Corleone immediately reminded me of him. Many more years later, Big Lou
confided that his father, who originally emigrated from Sicily
to New Orleans, got into a fight while working as a foreman
on a sugarcane plantation and killed a man with a cane knife.
His extended family sent him to Chicago to disappear into the
complexity of the big city. I've often wondered how I would
have felt about him if I had known about his dark past while
he was still alive. Would I have hated him? Feared him?
Romanticized his homicidal act? Occasionally he took the
commuter train to our house and stayed for breakfast or
lunch. His eating habits struck me as very strange. He put
ketchup on his eggs and ate a conglomeration of eggplant and
olives in a brown sauce for lunch.

That was all I knew of him.

He complained of stomach pains when he returned
from a trip to New Orleans. The doctor diagnosed his condition as food poisoning but later said he died of strangled bow-
els.

Big Lou walked into the house and asked, "What's
goin' on?"

"That was Angie on the phone," Mom answered.
"Poppa passed away."

His face didn't change. He maintained a quizzical
expression. When emotions overwhelmed him, he didn't
share them with us; he wouldn't even share them with himself. A scowl covered his feelings. He held his emotions
inside as if they were wild animals trying to escape. He
treated these overwhelming feelings with his own remedy, a
bottle of Seagram's 7. He poured himself a shot, sat at the
kitchen table with my mom, and downed the drink.

"What are the arrangements?" he asked showing no emotion.

"A '54 Plymouth Savoy," Dwayne declared as he squinted down 141st Street at a car so far away that it was hardly visible.

After Mike and I met Dwayne, *Name that Car* was never the same game. Dwayne always won. It was no longer a game; it was a class session on 1950s automobiles.

It was late Tuesday afternoon.

"I gotta' go," I said. "When my dad gets home from work, we're goin' to my grandfather's wake."

"What's a wake?" Mike asked.

"My mom said it's where people get together to remember and honor someone who died."

"It's where you go and look at a dead person," Dwayne added.

"No!" Mike and I returned in unison.

"Betcha'?"

First, we left Terri with my grandparents in Harvey. Then, Big Lou drove to 154th Street, the main street of Harvey, and parked the Nash. Several of my aunts, uncles, and people unknown to me stood outside the main door. They greeted us and some of the unknown people shook my father's hand and expressed their sympathy.

"Stay out here for a while with your cousins," Big Lou instructed Beth and me…then just to Beth and my older cousins, Kathy and Rae, and pointing at me, "Keep an eye on him."

After about an hour my father emerged from the building and called Beth and me. When we arrived, he took

us each by the hand and said, "It's time to say good-bye."
He led us through the heavy wooden main doors. The place
was like an old black-and-white movie cocktail party scene—
except no one had cocktails and everything was in color.
Several chandeliers lit the large room full of adults all dressed
up and clustered in small groups or seated on cushy ornate
sofas and chairs. They talked and laughed in low respectful
tones that produced a continuous somber murmur. Our father
led Beth and me through the murmuring crowd, across the
soft wine-colored carpet, between the pots and stands of
wreathes and bannered flower arrangements, and finally to a
priest kneeling on a wine-colored cushion with his head lowered in prayer. The priest stood, signed, and walked away; his
long black robe acted like a single theater curtain opening
and revealing the glimmering gold casket.

* * *

Tuesday, 8:55 p.m.
Several small groups of people mull in the funeral
parlor during the final hour of Mom's wake. Beth and Terri
mingle among the groups while I stand at the casket and greet
the last of the mourners.
An old man hobbles toward the casket. His handsome
dark blue suit and thin black-dyed hair can't disguise his
eighty-plus years. He squints at the coffin and mumbles as if
he is trying to remember something.
"Uncle John!" I smile and hold his shaky leathery
hand in both of mine. He is my mother's cousin, but we were
taught to refer to all adult relatives as "Uncle" or "Auntie."
When he looks at me his eyes widen into a bewildered stare.
"I'm Elsie's son, Uncle John. Remember? Pudgie?"

"Butchie? Butchie…Yes, Butchie!" He clasps his other hand over mine and shakes my hands in recognition. Then he squints again and whispers as if he is confiding a deep secret, "Listen…Butchie…I-57 north to the Dan Ryan Expressway—that'll get me back to the north side?"

I smile and wait; something else must be on his mind…there isn't.

"Yes, that's right, Uncle John."

He grins as if smiling pains his face, claps his hands over mine again, points toward my Uncle George (my mother's brother), and announces so everyone nearby can hear, "I'm gonna' go talk to your brother—George."

"You do that, Uncle John," I whisper. "You do that."

As he hobbles away, my fingers lightly brush against the coffin lid; it is dull and bronze—so unlike my grandfather's casket, or so my memory of it.

* * *

My father's strong hands lifted me high enough to view the top of the casket. In the middle of the open coffin, black beaded rosary snaked through my grandfather's pasty white sausage-like fingers. White cuffs with gold cufflinks protruded through the dark suit sleeves that led to his shoulders and face—his pale lifeless face. The obvious cosmetic effort to make him look so alive made it even more obvious that he was dead. They forgot to paint his thin smile. When we played outside the funeral home, people made comments as they left such as, "He looked so peaceful," "He looked just like himself," "Didn't he look like Lou?" But no one spoke the truth: He looked dead!

"Say good-bye to your grandfather, and you won't miss him so much," Big Lou whispered to me.

I started getting "that feeling"—shaky, sweaty, nervous, wanting to run. If I just close my eyes, I thought, I could get through this. But when I closed my eyes I saw Mr. Charleston's terrified, agonizing face. I writhed from my father's grasp and almost hit the casket before landing on the wine-colored carpet. I ran panic-stricken through the crowd and out the heavy wooden doors. My mother was close behind me, and when I turned and saw her I grabbed her around her legs, shook, and sobbed.

The doors opened, and two hands gently touched my shoulders. My Aunt Angie whispered to my mother, "I didn't know he and Poppa were that close."

Chapter 11

The rain finally let up enough so I could cross the alley and enter Mike's backyard through the white picket gate. On this mid-August morning, the black-gray sky blocked nearly all the sunlight; no doubt, it would rain all day. That had never bothered Mike or me, especially because on weekdays Mike's parents were away at work. Grandma Hale watched over Mike and the house during the day, but she kept to herself most of the time and left us alone.

Mike had a great imagination, much better than mine. The house became a hotel where two detectives solved murders, or a burning building that challenged the firemen of the TV show *Rescue 8*, or a TV western barroom brawl in the basement.

On this day, however, Mike's imagination stagnated. The TV was off, and he stared at the blank screen. Except when J.P lived with them and gave music lessons, the set always illuminated that room.

"Whatsa' matter?" I asked.

"Can't say," he said without emotion.

A long silence followed.

"What d'ya' wanta' do today?" I further inquired.

"Don't know." (Mike *always* had ideas.)

Another silence followed, so I tried a new tactic and asked, "You goin' on vacation tomorrow?" (A known fact.)

"Yeah."

"How long ya' gonna' be gone?"

"About two weeks" (Another known fact.)

Silence again.

"It's about Ellen Rae!" he finally confessed.

Ellen Rae lived in a house across the lane from Mike. She was a fifth-grader, and her features resembled the flute that she played in the Roosevelt School band. Slender and simple, she wore plain girls' winged glasses, perhaps to correct her turned-in right eye (the same reason that I wore glasses for my left eye). Although kids didn't ridicule her, neither did they visit her at home nor did they play with her.

The Roosevelt School band director required band members to attend lessons during the summer. One day while returning home from summer lessons, Ellen Rae had stopped to watch Mike and me wrestle on his front lawn.

"Bet I can beat both you guys," she said loud enough to stop our play.

We froze and stared. Our fathers forbade us to fight or wrestle with girls, and the neighborhood frowned on it. Nevertheless, this was a challenge, and Mike and I loved challenges.

"Okay," Mike answered, "me first."

Sure enough, she wrestled each of us and pinned us within seconds. This gave Ellen Rae our stamp of approval.

Her parents gave her numerous chores to do around the house, but her most enjoyable chore was gardening. She loved to plant, and Mike and I often helped her as she taught us gardening skills.

Her parents were English professors at the local junior college. Her father seemed to relish the position of "professor"; he sported a gray crew-cut and black-rimmed glasses. His sport coat and tie always seemed to be in motion as he briskly walked down the lane carrying his brown leather briefcase in one hand and an oversized textbook in the other.

"Good morning, young men," he greeted Mike and me. He neither waited nor expected a response; he rushed as if his presence somewhere else was of the utmost importance.

His wife carried herself with the same arrogance. She was a handsome woman, not as friendly as he, but more masculine.

Neighbors made attempts to converse with Ellen Rae's parents. During these conversations the learned professors often interrupted the small talk to correct their neighbors' grammar, so eventually no one talked to them.

"What about Ellen Rae?"

"Ya' gotta' promise not to tell anyone."

"I promise."

"Ya' sure ya' promise?"

"We're blood brothers, right? We picked our scabs and mixed our blood, didn't we?"

"Yesterday, before my mom and dad came home, I was playin' *Against the Steps*." *Against the Steps* was played with a rubber baseball and a fielder's glove. You threw the ball hard against the steps and tried to catch it when it bounced back to you. If it hit the edge of a step just right the ball flew over your head so you could make a spectacular catch. Occasionally the ball went in the wrong direction and would damage the front door screen; that's why you played *Against the Steps* when your parents were away. "It started to rain hard, so I went in our front screened-in porch 'til it stopped. Ellen Rae was trimmin' their front bushes, and she came into the porch, too, to get outa' the rain. So we was just sittin' there and Ellen Rae says, 'You know the difference between boys and girls?' I says, 'Sure.' She says, 'What?' I says, 'Girls got long hair and dresses. Boys don't.' She says, 'Naw, take your pants down.' I says, 'No!' but before I knew it, she pulled my pants and underpants down. I tried to pull 'em up, but she wouldn't let me. She says, 'See, boys got those and girls don't.' Then, she starts touchin' 'em with her hands!"

"No!"

"Yeah, and finally I get away and pull my pants up, and she comes over to me with a real mean look on her face, puts her finger in my face, and says, 'You better not tell any-one about this.' I says, 'I won't.' I was scared."

Mike exhaled as if he had just completed an arduous chore. We sat in silence for a long time. Neither Mike nor I knew anything about sex, but somehow we knew that what had happened to Mike was wrong.

"Ya gotta' tell your mom and dad," I said.

His relief disappeared. Fear and anxiety crept into his eyes again.

"I can't. I don't know what they'll say or do. What if they get mad, and what if they say we can't go on vacation?"

"Ya' gotta' tell 'em."

That day we played some board games. We played with our toy cars and tried to watch the Cubs game on TV, but it was rained out. Somehow, we just didn't feel like doing what we liked doing best on rainy days—imagining the house was the setting for an action TV show, and we were the main characters.

After dinner that evening the phone rang, and my mother answered it.

"Oh?...Oh!"

She moved from the dining area (where telephone conversations could be overheard) to the kitchen and talked in a muffled tone.

Big Lou sensed that something was wrong and moved from "his chair" in the living room to the kitchen. Beth, Terri, and I continued to watch TV. My mother hung up the phone and yelled, "Beth, take Terri and Pudge out front on the lane to play for a while!"

My parents frowned and sat opposite each other at the kitchen table. After several minutes, my father appeared at the front door and hollered through the screen, "Pudge! Come in here!"

He followed me with his eyes as I ran to the front door. He had an odd look on his face—almost as if he wasn't sure that he knew me anymore. I sat at the kitchen table, still littered with the gravy-stained plates and silverware. My mother now wore the same quizzical expression as my father. Neither parent seemed to know what to say. Finally, my mother began, "Pudge, when you and Mike played with Ellen Rae…did Ellen Rae…did Ellen Rae ever touch you?"

"What d'ya mean?" I asked naively, although I really knew what she meant.

"Did she ever touch your genitals?" Big Lou blurted.

"My what?"

This time I didn't know what he meant. My mother rolled her eyes at my father as if to say, "How the hell do you expect a kid his age to know what 'genitals' are!"

Big Lou clarified, "Did she ever touch you there?" He pointed to my crotch. "Did she ever pull your pants down, or have you pull your pants down?"

"No. No. Never."

Simultaneously, they sat back in their chairs and sighed.

"What's goin' on?" I asked.

"Never mind," my father answered, "but you and Mike are not to play with Ellen Rae anymore. Understood?"

"Yes, sir."

"Now go back out and play."

Mike and his family left for Florida the next day. The days passed slowly. I watched TV, tormented Beth and her friends, and occasionally put my *Roy Rogers* outfit on as I stalked bad guys throughout the neighborhood.

I knew his vacation would last approximately two weeks, but I didn't know the exact day of his return. Every morning of that second week, I climbed the concrete porch steps leading to his backdoor, knocked on the green screen door, and hoped someone would answer. On one of those days, I raised my fist to the screen door and heard a strange knocking even before my knuckles struck the green painted wood. From the raised concrete porch, I peered over the green hedges.

Ellen Rae's father stood on his front lawn. Knock. Knock. Knock. His hammer hit the long wooden stake that supported the brightly colored *For Sale* sign.

Chapter 12

Mike returned from his vacation late Sunday night; the next day was Labor Day. On Labor Day, 1957, Mike violated the unwritten, unspoken law of the neighborhood. It really wasn't his fault; his inexperience was to blame.

From early June through Labor Day kids respected this law: NEVER MENTION *IT* DURING THE SUMMER MONTHS. We didn't need to talk about *it;* reminders constantly warned us of *it.* The Ben Franklin five-and-dime store on 144th Street advertised "Back-to-*it*" supplies. Mothers discussed Back-to-*it* clothing sales. *It* even sent letters reminding parents to have their children vaccinated and registered before the first day of *it.*

Mike and I perched ourselves on separate black limbs of the strong cherry tree in my backyard. We grabbed bunches of the late summer black-red sour cherries, bit into the tight dark skin and moist flesh of each cherry, sucked the rich tart juice, and spat the pits onto the green lawn far below us. We knew that eating too many of these succulent sour cherries gave us sick stomachs, but we didn't care; we were lost in the moment...or so I thought.

"I can't wait!" Mike exploded. "I can't wait 'til tomorrow when schoo—I mean Clown Town starts! I wonder what my clown'll be like. I hope Ernie Banks comes on the first day…"

I couldn't believe it. I thought he had forgotten all about my fictitious Clown Town stories. He hadn't mentioned Clown Town all summer or even the last few months of the school year. My lies and guilt for telling those lies flooded every part of my body; it flushed my face, sweated my hands, and sickened my stomach—even more so than the cherries. He would find out the truth tomorrow—Clown Town was a fraud…and so was I.

"When Roy Rogers comes, I'm gonna'—"

"Mike!"

He looked up at me from a lower branch and anxiously waited.

"Mike…Ya' see…There's no…There's really no Clown Town…It's just…It's just school."

The anxious expression remained on his face for a few seconds as my words penetrated and destroyed his imagination. Slowly, his face reddened, and he breathed through his teeth as if his jaws were wired shut.

"I'm goin' home," he seethed as he slipped from his branch and shimmied down the tree.

"Wait! Mike!" I called and followed him.

He stomped across the lawn, through our picket gate, and into the alley.

"Sorry, Mike…I…just…"

He paused in the middle of the alley while I tried to apologize. Then, he picked up a rock and tossed it up and down a few times. I thought he might turn and throw it at me...I almost wished that he would. He, however, caught the rock in his palm, squeezed it so hard that his fist shook, wound up, and hurled it at his own white picket fence. The rock bounced high and hard off a fence board.

Mike sighed and strolled home like a pitcher who just walked in the winning run.

The rock had removed some of the pure white paint and exposed some bare pine. I touched my finger to the bare wood.

Chapter 13

I took off my glasses and wiped the smudges from the lenses with my shirttail. The playground echoed with the laughter and the screaming of the Park School baby boomers at recess. Over a hundred kids from first through third grade shared the playground during afternoon recess. Kindergartners didn't have recess, so I didn't see Mike at school.

It was almost October, and we hadn't played or spoken with each other since I had exposed the Clown Town myth on Labor Day. He was still mad about it and wouldn't talk to me. I missed our friendship, but I made some new friends in the first grade. I called them my baseball buddies because we traded baseball cards and played baseball during recess and after school in the park.

Jentz was the leader. With his short blond hair and quick laughter, he was a pudgy version of Mike. Jentz exercised his unique talent for handing out nicknames that stuck for years. I became Macaroni, later shortened to Mac. A tall athletic baseball buddy became Lolly, from the comic strip *Lolly and Pepper,* later shortened to Loll. Mueller, another tall and studious baseball buddy, became Pueller, later shortened to Pues. The biggest, strongest, and toughest baseball buddy, Smith, became Smitty Babe, later shortened to Smitty, and later shortened to the Babe.

While cleaning my glasses I gazed at the three female teachers conversing on the sidewalk that bordered the school building and the green grass of the huge playground. Two of them, including my teacher, were young and pretty; Mrs. Caruso, the third-grade teacher, was not. All of them carried shiny stainless steel whistles on a chain around their necks for the purpose of signaling the end of recess or "foul play."

* * *

Wednesday, 2:32 a. m.

"Damn!" My heel slams against the dark oak footboard of our bed. I wake up in a sitting position.

Dorinda quickly clicks on her overhead bed lamp fixed to the wall.

"What's wrong?"

"I don't know…I…must have been dreaming."

"What were you dreaming about?"

"I really can't remember. Go back to sleep. I'm all right."

She flicks off the light, plops her head onto her pillow, and fades off to sleep.

I lie and stare at the ceiling fan. Remembering dreams has never been my strong point. I am angry and confused—confused because I don't know why I'm angry.

As my mind and body relax, a thought occurs to me: a teacher institute seminar, several years ago, "Helping Teens Cope with Grief," the seven stages of grieving—Denial, Guilt, Anger…, or was it Anger and then Guilt? What's the difference? Some Ph.D. speaker said, "Anger is a natural stage of the grieving process…"

So now I feel comfortable with my anger; strangely, I even feel nostalgic about it.

Dorinda's shiny black hair rivals the darkness in the room. The long strands spread like a fan against her bright white pillow.

* * *

Without my glasses, my turned-in left eye became much more visible. Three third-grade boys stood nearby. The biggest third grader, Ron, pointed to me and said to the other two, "Look at that cock-eyed kid!"

All three laughed.

Anger swelled inside of me—the same way it had over a year earlier when Miss Hickey ridiculed me in front of the class. But this time I didn't laugh with them; I threw down my glasses, charged Ron, and grabbed him around his legs. Because he was bigger than I, he didn't take my attack seriously and said something like, "C'mon, kid. Give it up," but I wasn't finished. Years of wrestling with Mike had taught me some moves. I wrapped my left ankle behind his and drove his body in that direction. As he lost balance and tumbled backwards, his arms reached back to break his fall. That's when my arms and fists twirled hard against his face that spat warm sticky blood onto my knuckles.

Ron turned onto his stomach, quickly drew his knees up, and stood. His face flared with anger and his fists clenched tightly; he knew now that he was in a fight, and he would avenge the humiliation of getting bloodied by a first grader.

My mind wouldn't acknowledge the sounds—the kids yelling, "Fight! Fight!" or the shrill whistles warning, "Foul play!" I took several hard punches to the sides of my head to get one good punch into his stomach that doubled him over and allowed me to hit him square in the face again. As he fell backwards, I climbed up his legs and readied for another assault. That's when I felt the big male hands of Max, the janitor, the only male adult in the small primary school building; he pulled me off Ron and ushered me toward the building. The three teachers attended to Ron, who appeared to be more bloodied than I.

As Max steered me toward the building, Mary, a pretty green-eyed little girl with long wavy black hair, stepped in front of us.

"Here, Louis, I think these are yours."

She held out my yellow-rimmed glasses in her small delicate hand. When I reached for my glasses, my dirty bloody hand touched hers. She didn't even pull away or say, "Yechh!"

I would forever have a certain fondness for fighting and black-haired girls.

Chapter 14

The Park School secretary looked like Humphrey Bogart in a dress. Bogart could have only dreamed of being that macho.

"Louis, you and your parents can have a seat here until Mrs. Bennett arrives."

Three days had passed since the fight. Immediately after, the Park School teachers had called Mrs. Bennett for direction. Mrs. Bennett, the principal of the elementary school district, kept her office at the main school building, Roosevelt School, about a mile away. She suspended me by telephone and set up a meeting with my parents and me for the morning of my return.

After the fight my mother had picked me up from school and sent me to my room until Big Lou came home from work. As soon as he came home, the grilling began.

"Why did you attack that boy?" my mother asked.

"He called me cross-eyed or cock-eyed or somethin' like that."

My father's eyes widened as he formed a subtle smile, but he forced it into a frown for my mom's benefit.

"Was he bigger than you?" Big Lou asked.

"Yeah, he was a third-grader."

He almost beamed, so he left my room and let my mother handle the rest. She lectured me on how everyone is different, and we shouldn't let others anger us so much that we lowered ourselves to the point of fighting. She reminded me that the glasses would eventually straighten my eye, and I wouldn't need to be so sensitive about it.

I promised her that I wouldn't fight anymore, but I really didn't know if I could keep that promise.

Mrs. Bennet arrived within minutes. She carried herself with an air of confidence that made her seem taller than her average height. Her dark business outfit, long skirt and matching short jacket, announced that she was all business. The short red scarf with a bow at the side tied tightly around her neck reminded us that she was a woman, also. Although not particularly pretty, her handsome weathered face coupled with her graying dark hair hinted at her long experience and her sense of justice and fair play.

"Hello, I'm Mrs. Bennett and you must be Louis's parents," she said as she extended her hand and smiled.

She led us behind the secretary's desk to a very small conference room housing a round table and four chairs. My parents and I sat down first. Mrs. Bennett seated herself and got right to business. "Well, Louis, you were fighting. Why?"

I explained what had happened, and she listened intently. When I finished, she asked my parents some questions about my eye condition. Following their answers, she essentially gave me the same lecture my mother had given me. My mother focused all her attention on Mrs. Bennett's words and often nodded her approval. Big Lou stared at the shiny yellow enameled cinder block walls and probably thought, "How the hell do they heat this place?"

Mrs. Bennett turned to my parents. "Louis obviously has a problem controlling his temper. This isn't uncommon for a child who somehow feels different from the others. Louis, you must learn to control your temper."

"Yes, ma'am."

"You hurt Ronny badly. You don't want to hurt people, do you?"

"No, ma'am."

That was a lie; I did want to hurt Ron. In a twisted way, she had just declared me the winner, and that felt good.

"Are you sorry for fighting, and will you control your temper from now on?"

"Yes, ma'am."

"Let's hear you say it." My father finally spoke.

"I won't fight, and I'll control my temper."

"Well, Louis, you seem like you're a smart young man, and your parents are very supportive, so I'm going to let you return to your class. But keep in mind, if you continue to fight and to lose your temper, I will have to put you into a special classroom for students who have trouble controlling their tempers."

My mother gasped, but Mrs. Bennett smiled and shook her head as if to say, "I doubt that we will have to take that measure."

I, however, wasn't so confident. I wasn't even sure what a "temper" meant. To me, a temper was like a wild animal inside of me. I knew that Big Lou had a temper inside of him, and I knew how he controlled it. Whenever the wild animal stirred, he locked it down tightly. The animal beat against his insides, produced a scowl on his reddening face, and churned his stomach. He would walk around and shake his scowling face until the animal gave up and left him tired and weak. Sometimes he would use beer or whiskey to calm the animal, but he was careful not to rely on that too often. Occasionally, the wild animal escaped, and my father would lash out violently with words or fists. However, after the animal was gone, Big Lou always apologized for losing control.

I didn't want the wild animal beating up my insides; I was too young to drink, and if I let the wild animal escape, they'd put me in a class with a bunch of crazies, I thought.

When I returned to my classroom Mrs. Allen said, "Welcome back, Louis. Have a seat and take out your *Numbers* book." All eyes focused on me as I walked to my desk, and the low murmur of whispering began.

Chapter 15

"T-h-th-e the d-d-o-o-g-ga dog ra-a-na ran u-u-p up the ha-i-i-la hill. The dog ran up the hill."

On October 14th, 1957, I read that sentence aloud in class. On that day, the symbols became sounds; the sounds became words; the words became a sentence; and the sentence became an image. Wow! I thought, I can read!

Neither temper tantrums nor fights threatened my stay in the classroom. Word had gotten out that the little guy wearing glasses could fight. Hanging around with my baseball buddies protected me, also. No one knew if Loll could fight or not, but his athletic stature and size insured that no one wanted to find out. Everyone knew that Smitty had a temper worse than mine and that he could take on the whole third grade if he wanted.

This protective environment allowed me to concentrate on school and to discover the joy of reading. I practiced sounding out words on print material at home and on signs and billboards when we rode in the Nash.

By Halloween, my mother bragged to neighbors about my constant reading practice, and Big Lou was ready to tape my mouth shut and throw me into the Little Calumet River.

The teacher assigned us to one of three reading groups depending on her judgment of our reading ability. The *Tom and Betty* group contained the "challenged" readers. Parents earned bragging rights if their child entered the prestigious *Alice and Jerry* group of "accelerated" readers. Despite all my reading practice, the teacher placed me in the *Dick and Jane* group, the mediocre readers.

* * *

Wednesday, 6:20 a.m.

The dogs and I sit and enjoy the morning rays streaming through the windows in our semi-circular sunroom. I'm told that during the 1920s, when our home was built, the family waked their deceased loved ones here. Visitors gathered in the "living" room, adjacent to the sunroom.

The funeral home will host services for Mom at 10:00 a.m. before the procession to the cemetery.

I awoke at 4:30 to feed the dogs and couldn't go back to sleep, so I'm dressed and ready, almost four hours early. Perhaps my mysterious nightmare shook me into this sleepless state.

Whenever I feel edgy, reading somehow relaxes me. The words lead me into my imagination where I am safe and comfortable. I open my current book, *This Boy's Life* by Tobias Wolf—page 201, *"...I never knew whether he felt the same way. In most respects we were strangers. But it mattered to me that he was my brother, and it seemed to matter to him..."*

* * *

The class silently read from their primers after individual reading group instruction. The plot of my silent reading story concerned Dick, Jane, their dog Spot, and their younger sister, whose name I can never force myself to remember, meeting with a group of friends to go trick-or-treating. I sadly thought about Mike and me; we went trick-or-treating every year in the costumes our mothers had invented. Later, we emptied our bags and sorted the mounds of colorfully wrapped candy.

After reading the story, I closed my book, folded my arms over my desk, lay my head on my arms, shut my eyes, and missed my friend.

Chapter 16

My small fist hadn't knocked on Mike's back door in over two months. After my signature three loud knocks and a short wait, the big white inside backdoor swung open.

Mike stood alone and faced me through the screen. I opened the screen door and placed my foot inside like Jack Webb on *Dragnet* forcing his way into a suspect's house.

"You still mad at me?" I asked in my most innocent voice.

For a moment, he just stared. His smile spread like the long-awaited curtain opening of a musical play.

"Naw! C'mon in!"

I followed him toward the TV room.

Mike had formed at least one new friendship during my absence. A strong wiry-looking kid in a plain white T-shirt and jeans sat on a wooden chair and laughed in short tense heaves as he pounded the armrests and focused on the TV screen.

"Hey, Rick. This is Pudge."

Rick glanced over, still laughing, and exclaimed, "Hey, Pudge! Hey, you guys, ya' gotta' watch this! This is great!"

He was watching professional wrestling. The tag team match featured Big Gene Koniecski and Killer Kowalski versus Edwar Carpentier and Good Boy Floyd. The match degenerated into a brawl that extended outside the ring and into the audience. Folding chairs and phony punches flew everywhere, and we bought it all. Intermittently, Rick, with his mouth wide open and his eyes ready to pop out, turned to Mike and me and a deep nearly inaudible laugh hoarsely erupted from his throat while his head nodded as if his forehead were a hammerhead pounding in a nail.

I liked Rick. His dare-devil attitude and constant quest for fun made him a natural mutual friend for Mike and me. This proved especially convenient since Dwayne, our other mutual friend, attended the Catholic school, so we rarely saw him during the school year. Rick and Mike were classmates; all three of us were close in age, physical size, and boyhood interests.

Rick lived on LaSalle Street with his mother, father, older sister, younger sister, and younger brother. They had moved to Riverdale in the fall so that his father could join the Riverdale Police Department.

"Hey!" Mike announced. "Me and Rick are goin' to the Dolton Show later ta' see some movies. Wanna' come?"

"Sure, if I can," I answered.

"That's cool," Rick said. "Hey, look. The bald guy's crack is showin'."

Marion dropped us off at the Dolton Theater twenty minutes before the show started. Kids, mostly teenagers, packed the tiny theater.

Previews of coming attractions included scenes from a new Disney film, *Old Yeller*. "Coming Christmas day," the announcer informed. Mike and I loved dogs and vowed to see this movie over Christmas break. Rick didn't care much for dogs or the movie previews, during which a pimply-faced teenage usher dressed in his uniform of a white shirt, black bowtie, and red double-breasted jacket walked down the aisle and waved the beam of his flashlight randomly around the theater.

"Hey! You guys wanna' stop throwin' popcorn!" his cracking puberty voice warned.

"We're not throwin' popcorn, crater-face," a voice shouted back from the darkness.

"What'd you call me?" the usher yelled back and shined his flashlight in that general direction.

"You wanna' shut the hell up, so we can hear the movie!" a voice cried from the darkness of another part of the theater.

"You shut up, or I'll kick your ass otta' here!" returned the usher as he tried to locate the source with his flashlight.

"My ass and your face, a perfect match!" a voice retorted from the darkness.

Rick leaned forward—his face between the seats in front of him. "Does your ass have pimples, too?" he said; then quickly sat back in his seat.

The usher focused his beam of light directly on the kid seated in front of Rick. "You're otta' here!" he screamed, pulled the kid from his seat, and ushered him out the door.

We didn't care much for the first movie, *Loving You* starring Elvis Presley. Every time Elvis appeared on the screen, a group of teenage girls screamed and drowned the dialogue. We liked one scene: A tough guy walks up to Elvis in a diner and demands that Elvis sing a song for his girlfriend. When Elvis refuses, the guy punches him, and Elvis beats the snot out of him. Then Elvis plugs a nickel into the jukebox and sings *Teddy Bear* to the guy's girlfriend anyway. To us, that was like a pitcher knocking down a batter with a fastball. Then the batter stands up and hits a homerun on the next pitch.

The scene left me confused, however. After losing his temper and getting into a fight, Elvis emerged the cool guy. When I lost my temper and fought, I emerged dirty, bloody, suspended, and threatened to be thrown out of school. Elvis's temper was a *teddy bear*, not a wild animal as I had imagined.

> *I don't wanna be a tiger,*
> *Cuz tigers play too rough.*
> *I don't wanna be a lion,*
> *Cuz lions aren't the kind*
> *You love enough.*
> *I just wanna be*
> *Your teddy bear.*

If the first movie almost convinced me that a temper was a teddy bear, the second movie confirmed my former belief. A young Michael Landon starred in the sci-fi horror classic *I Was a Teenage Werewolf*. Landon played a teenager who struggled with the effects of having a hot temper. He sees a doctor about his problem; however, the doctor isn't a psychiatrist as Landon had thought; he's a mad scientist who hypnotizes Landon and gives him some potion that turns him into a werewolf every time his temper flares. After several terrifying killing sprees that turned the theater into a dark box of high-pitched screams, Landon confronts the doctor. The doctor provokes Landon, and Landon transforms into the werewolf. The werewolf kills the doctor just as the local police are closing in on him. Police bullets kill the werewolf who transforms back into a dead teenage Michael Landon.

"The End," and the theater lights brightened. Mike and Rick traded looks of elation.

"Great movie!" they summarized.

"Hey, Pudge! You still look scared," remarked Rick.

"I am, Rick. I am."

The cold December wind blew thin sheets of snow onto the freshly shoveled sidewalks and streets and mocked the human effort to keep the concrete clean. The day after Christmas was supposed to be a joyous day, a day when kids played and shared the toys and games they had received on Christmas day. Mike and I spent the morning doing just that. However, the afternoon winter darkness at 5:30 equaled the darkness of midnight, and we stood shivering in front of the Dolton Theater. Our reddened eyes hurt from salty tears. Those salty tears burned our eyes until we could hold them in no longer and they streamed down our faces and embarrassed us. The movie spoiled the joys of the previous day.

About two hours earlier we sat in the theater and watched the movie that we had waited nearly two months to see, *Old Yeller.* Most of the film met our expectations and more. Two boys befriend a faithful lovable golden retriever, Yeller. The film chronicled the adventures of the three friends. Yeller protects the boys by fighting a wolf, but he contracts a disease from the wolf bites. The disease turns Yeller into a vicious "mad dog," and the older boy must make a heartbreaking decision. He sticks the mussel of his rifle into the cage of Yeller, now a wild animal, and shoots him.

My eyelids shut tightly at the sound of the gunshot. When they opened, tears gushed from them and streaked down my cheeks. This contradicted the manly skill of hiding my feelings that Big Lou had been teaching me by his example. I stared stoically at the screen and hoped that Mike didn't notice my humiliating display; but when I finally turned to face him, his seat was empty.

In a panic I ran to the lobby. The seductive smell of hot buttered popcorn permeated the air and the pimply-faced usher leaned on the glass candy counter and bored the refreshment stand girl. Through the glass exit doors the light from tiny bulbs surrounding the movie promotional posters reflected off Mike; he stood on the sidewalk and sobbed uncontrollably.

I passed through the exit doors and stood silently behind him. I empathized with his pain and envied his willingness to release it. The strange silence made me contemplate my own feelings. I felt sorrow for Yeller, but I felt sorrow for myself, also. Another movie confirmed that a mad dog, a wild animal, a temper, must die, even if the killer loves it.

I placed my hand on one of Mike's heaving shoulders.

Across the street a German shepherd walked silently in the snow and into the light of the corner streetlamp. He sniffed at a small mound of shoveled snow next to the light pole. His front paws busily burrowed into the mound of snow in search of something that his sensitive sense of smell promised worthy. His burrowing stopped, and his eyes stared with disappointment at the source of the promising scent.

He trotted from the streetlamp's illuminated circle and into the silent darkness of the night.

Chapter 17

Boredom must have made me flick the orange piece of chalk with my thumb, and it spun like a propeller atop my clean and polished desktop. Mrs. Allen spoke slowly and clearly when she gave directions for our art assignment, but she may as well have spoken in Russian. My body sat at attention, but my mind vacationed in the memories of the previous two weeks of Christmas break.

The janitors had cleaned, polished, and waxed away the Christmas atmosphere—except for the miniature decorated Christmas tree that Mrs. Allen had forgotten to bring home. It stood on the windowsill against the long row of frosted windows. Nothing is more depressing, I thought, than Christmas decorations that are left up too long after the holidays.

Teachers dreaded this first day back to school as much as we did, and they were unprepared to teach. They kept us busy with easy, long, and meaningless assignments while they organized and prepared lessons for the remainder of the week.

My mind drifted aimlessly. I began fearing my own irrational thoughts—thoughts about losing my temper and getting placed into a "special" class or being shot like Michael Landon or Yeller. My protection had worn thin with time. People forgot about my fight earlier in the school year, and soon someone would tease me about my crossed eye. My baseball buddies were tough and loyal, but they were smart, also. They wouldn't risk getting suspended from school over a fight to protect me.

No one except Pues had been listening to Mrs. Allen's directions, so when she left the room to get coffee, he re-taught the class. "We're 'spose ta' use these colored pieces of chalk and construction paper ta' draw somethin' that reminds us of our Christmas vacation."

My blank construction paper stared up at me and dared me to fill it as I continued to spin the chalk pieces on my desktop. My imagination filled the space with various vacation thoughts: the fierce snowball fight after the last school day before break; the day we brought the Scotch pine Christmas tree into the house and decorated it; my Christmas present, the Lionel electric train set circling the tree on Christmas morning; the sound of the rifle when Yeller got shot; the pimply-faced usher trying to impress the candy counter girl; Mike crying outside the theater; the German shepherd beneath the streetlamp.

Perhaps I was just lazy, but none of those images inspired me enough to start drawing.

I thought about the previous day, Sunday. I had successfully faked a stomachache and avoided going to Sunday school. The family left for church, and my mother ordered me to stay in bed until they returned. As soon as they left, I ran downstairs and turned on the TV set. Channels 2, 5, and 7 (the network stations) broadcasted dull news shows such as *Meet the Press.* The local station, channel 9 WGN, featured *Flash Gordon,* formerly a 1930s movie serial of the Aryan-looking Flash riding around in his spaceship trying to save a buxom blond from the evil Merciless Ming. I watched for about ten minutes until the commercial break. Earl Sheib, a shifty-looking local businessman, always bought this cheap Sunday morning commercial spot.

"I'm Earl Scheib, and I'll paint any car any color for just $19.99..."

Click, click. I forwarded the dial to channel 11, the Public Broadcasting Station. A documentary on silent movie comics snared my attention. The narration didn't interest me, but the clips from the movies of Charlie Chaplin, Fatty Arbuckle, Buster Keaton, Laurel and Hardy, and Harold Lloyd forced long and painful belly laughs from me. Then a comic appeared whom I had never seen before; his name was Ben Turpin. His right eye crossed inward, the same as my left eye. I imagined a theater full of people roaring with laughter when the camera held a close-up of his face, but I didn't laugh. It was as if the close-up shot was on me, and the imag-inary audience was laughing at me, also. My dormant temper grew inside of me. Strangely, however, I smiled, chuckled, and then laughed until I could hardly breathe. Ben Turpin's slapstick and comic timing produced more laughter than the laughter produced from a crossed eye. I felt as if I were laughing at both him and myself.

* * *

Wednesday, 9:05 a.m.

My thirty-three-year-old cousin's new metallic blue Ford glimmers in the sunlight; it is the only car parked in the funeral home lot when we arrive. He is one of my six cousins who will serve as a pallbearer today. The funeral director wanted them there early for instructions.

Dorinda stops to chat with my cousin's wife in the lobby.

My cousin sits in the lounge and stares at a floor tile. His young daughters draw stick figures on a small standing blackboard that the funeral director set up in a corner for kids. He was close to my mother; like many family members, he often turned to her for advice and support.

I sit next to him, but he still gazes at the tile as if he were hypnotized.

"So, these two ninety-year-old men are sittin' on a couch in an old folks' home…"

His eyes remain transfixed, but his mouth stretches into a broad toothy smile as he recognizes the familiar cadence to the beginning of one of my crude jokes.

"One guy turns to the other and says, 'Man this gettin' old is a bitch. Sometimes it takes me almost half an hour just to urinate.' The other guy nods and says, 'I know what ya' mean. Sometimes it takes me an hour just to have a bowel movement.' Another old guy passing them in his walker overhears their conversation and says, 'Gentlemen, I'm one hundred-years-old, and every morning, nine o'clock sharp, I piss like a racehorse; a few minutes later, I crap like a cow!' The ninety-year-old guys say, 'Gee, that's great!' The hundred-year-old shakes his head, shuffles away, and says, 'Not really. I don't get up 'til ten.'

My cousin explodes with laughter.

His daughters mimic him and continue drawing stick figures.

* * *

"Everyone doing alright?" Mrs. Allen sang as she strolled back into the classroom and sipped her coffee. Without looking for a response, she set her cup of coffee onto her desk, walked to the blackboard, and wrote with a piece of chalk.

I took off my glasses, closed my eyes, and rubbed the corners of them along the bridge of my nose in response to a headache. When my eyes opened, they focused on the rhythmical movements of Mrs. Allen's butt as she wrote on the blackboard. I was too young to know why her movements fascinated me, but I watched with enjoyment anyway.

Two girls whispered to each other, glanced at me and giggled. I knew that they were giggling at my crossed left eye. The wild animal within me stirred, and I feared that I would say or do something crazy leading me to trouble. I put my glasses upside down over my eyes, stuck my tongue out to the side, pushed my ears forward, and stared at the girls. They covered their mouths and giggled audibly. Mrs. Allen turned from the blackboard and glared at them. The girls stopped giggling and quickly returned to their work. I righted my glasses and pretended to draw. Mrs. Allen shrugged her shoulders and turned toward the blackboard. The two girls glanced back at me. I returned an exaggerated innocent look and shrugged my shoulders, mocking Mrs. Allen's gesture. The girls covered their mouths and giggled again

My feelings amazed me—no anger, no temper, no wild animal inside me. I felt happy; I felt in control.

I picked up a piece of chalk and began to draw a happy, beautiful, and colorful clown.

Chapter 18

Mr. Saliba, the president of the Board of Education, stood like a Nazi barracks inspector in the doorway of the classroom on this frigid mid-February morning.

"Good morning, young people!" he bellowed in a phony deep voice that he apparently used to compensate for his diminutive stature. His bushy, dark, narrow mustache covered his upper lip, and his black-rimmed glasses framed his small squinty eyes. Thin brown hair combed over from just above his ear tried to hide his wide bald head, but the cold February wind parted the masking hairs and revealed his shiny skull. His opened overcoat revealed a bargain-basement dark suit and his short-cuffed pants exposed his white socks and brown dress shoes.

Wisecracks raced from my brain to my vocal chords, but I choked them down and buried my head in work.

Mrs. Allen had prepared the class for his annual visit to Park School. She told us that he would be evaluating her by our performance in the classroom. Since the class really liked Mrs. Allen, every child behaved and performed like 50s TV child actors.

His visit tested me, also. Since early January, I had established myself as the class clown. I cracked up students

during both silent and oral reading; I disrupted the class occasionally, and worst of all, my grades and progress dropped
dramatically.

Mrs. Allen, however, proved to be a very clever
teacher. She neither called my parents, invoked disciplinary
measures, nor created a "me versus her" confrontation. She
recognized my sense of humor and need for attention, so she
designated the last hour of class as "Entertainment Hour,"
every Friday. Her rule stated that students could perform
before the class if those students behaved admirably during
that week.

Several students played musical instruments while
others sang solos or duets to a critical crowd of first-graders.
I made up my mind to stop disrupting class during the week
and save my clowning for "Entertainment Hour."

My "Entertainment Hour" debut was a smash. The
class laughed and cheered when I finished the comedy routine I had memorized from *The Red Skelton Show* on TV the
previous Tuesday night. Everyone's laugh reflected his/her
personality. Jentz's was a spontaneous, uninhibited, "ha-ha"
that neither he nor a teacher could ever stop or control. Loll
laughed without a sound; just a wide grin froze on his face.
Pues had a deep, dignified, intellectual laugh; if one could
imagine Abe Lincoln laughing—that was Pues. Smitty had
the most unique and contagious laugh of all. He would cover
his mouth with his hand as if he were about to throw up.
From the depths of his huge body a tremendous honking
sound erupted from his mouth which blew his large hand
away. His laugh sounded like a foghorn mating with a two-
hundred-pound goose. Mrs. Allen's laugh scared us. Her
face reddened as her entire body shook, and her shoulders

heaved up and down. She seemed to gasp for air while her fist pounded on a flat surface. Laughter amplified her attractive features: large gentle eyes, and a young shapely figure.

"Class, this is Mr. Saliba, the president of the Board of Education," Mrs. Allen announced. "Welcome, Mr. Saliba."

"Thank you, Mrs. Allen. Well, I see your young scholars are busy at work. That's good to see. Good to see. When I was your age, we didn't have nice warm classrooms like you have in the winter. It was the Depression, you know. Our classroom was heated with one tiny wood-burning stove. We walked to school many miles in the cold weather, and we didn't have warm coats and mittens like you have. You should be thankful. Yes. Yes. Well, carry on, Mrs. Allen. Good-bye, and be thankful, young people. Be thankful!"

He turned abruptly on the heels of his Buster Brown dress shoes and walked with swift short steps toward the building exit doors. He drove away in his shiny new Edsel, and since I sat next to the row of windows, all eyes focused in my direction; I couldn't resist the captive audience. I pulled my pant legs above my knees, took a black comb from my pocket, covered half the comb's teeth with my hand, positioned it below my nose, and mocked, "Good morning, young people! I walked to school twenty miles in the deep snow. I was bare-butt naked. You should be thankful. Yes. Yes."

Smitty's signature honk signaled the rest of the class to laugh. I realized that I might be in trouble and turned toward Mrs. Allen.

Behind her desk she gasped for air between laughs and pounded her fists on the shiny gray floor tiles.

Chapter 19

A single dot of light...

Within the thick blackness of the room only a single dot of light shined directly on my left eye.

"Try not to look at the light, Louis, and look straight ahead," Dr. Daley ordered and probed the ray from his hand-held instrument around my left eye. He clicked off the tiny light, and for a brief moment the smothering blackness set a panic throughout my body. Dr. Daley flicked the switch on and as my eyes adjusted to the brightness the panic disappeared. The sterile white walls, the familiar eye chart hanging on the wall, and the huge leather examining chair reminded me that I was in Dr. Daley's eye examining room.

My mother sat in a metal folding chair against the wall. Dr. Daley turned on his cushy swivel chair and wrote on my open medical file. For several minutes the only sound was that of Dr. Daley's pen marking my file, his heavy breathing, and his occasional humming of the song *Count Your Blessings*.

Just a thick patch of dull gray hair half-circled his ears and huge bald head that glowed from the bright fluorescent lights above. As he looked through the bottom portion of the thick lenses of his bifocals, I thought, why would an eye doctor wear such thick-lensed glasses? Shouldn't his eyes be perfect?

He turned on his swivel chair, completely ignored me, faced my mother directly, and whispered to her, "The glasses just aren't working well enough. Let's you and I talk in my office."

With a worried expression, my mother followed him out the door.

"I'll be right back," she lied as the door closed, and I sat alone in the bright sterile room. I wondered, am I invisible?

After sitting alone for half an hour, I imagined the worst: "I'm afraid," my imaginary Dr. Daley said to my mother, "that we cannot help your son. I'm sorry, but we will have to shoot him."

The door opened and my mother appeared. She seemed less worried.

"Ready to go?" she asked me.

Dumb question.

"Thank you so much, Dr. Daley," my mother said to him, "and I will contact him."

"Well, good luck to you." He smiled at her and completely ignored me, again.

As she backed the Nash out the parking space, I asked, "What's goin' on!"

She hit the brakes as if my presence suddenly startled her. She sighed and said confidently, "We'll talk about it after the wedding."

* * *

Wednesday, 9:38 a.m.

The assistant funeral director, a young portly man who takes his job seriously, distributes thin gray gloves to my six cousins/pallbearers. They take turns rolling their eyes behind his back as he spews detailed instructions as if they were toddlers.

A few elderly people have arrived early and seat themselves in the funeral service room. They smile at me, and I return a nod and a grin even though I don't recognize them.

I peruse the collage of photographs my sisters created; it's attractively displayed on an easel among the plants and flower arrangements. One snapshot, however, disturbs me. It had been taken at Dorothy and Ray's wedding reception. My father and mother are standing on the bandstand. Beth, Terri, and I are seated at their feet. Everyone is dressed up; everyone is smiling—except me. I stare expressionless through my yellow-rimmed glasses at something off-camera.

* * *

The wedding.

The next day, Saturday, March 8th, Dorothy and Ray married at Peace United Church of Christ in Harvey, a half-block from my grandparents' home. I remember very little of the ceremony except that Ray looked totally out of place in his dark tuxedo, white cumber bun, and white bowtie. This wasn't the Ray who dressed in his James Dean rolled-up short-sleeved collar-up sport shirt and recklessly drove Beth and me in his '57 Chevy to drive-ins and Dairy Queens. Nevertheless, when Ray, standing with his groomsmen in the front of the church, caught sight of me sitting in a front pew, he smiled and mouthed, "Hey, Big Jim."

"A seven-and-seven, a beer, and—," I had to think for a moment, "and a martini."

"Good man!" my Uncle George exclaimed, slapped the top of the green painted wooden bar in the American Legion Hall, and began to make the drinks. My Uncle George (my mother's brother), my father, and two of his brothers volunteered to tend bar at the reception. My father volunteered me to deliver drink orders.

It was a great job. I basked in the attention of the adults, especially the young women in their tight-fitting cocktail dresses. More importantly, they stuffed the pockets of my gray suit with generous tips, and the more they drank, the more they tipped.

Uncle George arranged the three drinks on the round blue metal *Pabst Blue Ribbon Beer* tray.

"Okay, Pudge, take her away and be careful."

I balanced the tray of drinks and cut across the dance floor. The three-piece band was really good; they mainly played rock and roll, and as they started *Hound Dog* couples rushed to the dance floor. The dancers parted so that I could pass, and I heard comments such as, "Doesn't he look cute in that little gray suit?"

As I made my way through the crowd I looked for the three elderly women who had ordered the drinks. Two of them stood in front of the ladies' room. Both had white hair. One wore a long flowered dress. The other wore a light-colored crinkly see-through gown, but I didn't think anyone wanted to see through it.

I delivered the drinks.

The flowered dress woman took the martini. The see-through lady took the other two drinks. "Thank you, dear," she said. "The seven-and-seven is for Alice. She's in the ladies' room. I'll hold it for her."

No tip.

Oh well, I thought, I'll take a little break and watch the dancers for a while. My Uncle Sam, my father's brother, was cracking up his dance partner and the dancers around him. He was lanky and reminded me of Art Carney's character, Ed Norton, of *The Honeymooners*. He rock and rolled wildly and wide-eyed just as Ed Norton might have danced.

The other elderly lady, a blue-haired woman, returned from the ladies' room and took her drink. I turned from them and continued to watch the dancers.

"Isn't that Lou and Elsie's boy?" I overheard one of them say.

"Yes, did you notice his bad left eye; it's crossed," the blue-haired woman remarked.

"Really?"

"Uh-huh," the blue-haired woman continued, "and I overheard Elsie telling her mother that they were taking him to a specialist, and he may have to undergo surgery."

"Really?"

I almost dropped my *Pabst Blue Ribbon* metal tray. A specialist? Surgery? And these old hags knew about it before I knew? The tray shook in my hand; I felt my dormant temper kindle, but almost as a reflex I felt my recently acquired sense of humor flare, also.

I turned and surveyed the three women. That's when I noticed something and remarked respectfully, "Ma'am, are you taking that home with you?"

"What's that, young man?"

"That piece of toilet paper you dragged from the bathroom; it's stuck to your shoe."

"Ahh!" she screamed as she spilled her drink and tried to remove the tissue from her high heel.

I began my journey across the dance floor toward the bar.

They said you was high classed
Well, that was just a lie.
Yeah, they said you was high classed
Well, that was just a lie.
Well, you ain't never caught a rabbit,
You ain't no friend of mine.

Chapter 20

"What's this about surgery on my eye?" I asked my mother on Sunday morning.

We had arrived home late from the wedding reception Saturday night. Everyone but my mother and I slept in the next morning. When I heard my mother get out of bed to make coffee and breakfast, I came downstairs to confront her about what I had heard from the old ladies' conversation. I didn't bring it up at the wedding because I didn't want to spoil everyone's good time.

My mother stared at me as if I had asked her where babies came from.

"Where did you hear that?"

"A blue-haired woman heard you tellin' Grandma about it."

She stared into the air as she tried to recall who may have overheard her talking to my grandmother. Something registered, and she nodded to herself.

"Well," she sighed and now focused on me, "we were going to talk to you about it, but first I had to talk to your father and see if our insurance covered the cost. Dr. Daley thinks that this other doctor, a specialist, might be able to straighten your eye. You wouldn't need glasses anymore, but you would have to have an operation. We wanted to tell you the right way, so you wouldn't be scared."

Scared, I thought? Scared? Why would I be scared? My eye would be straight, no more glasses. An operation? Mike had had an operation two years earlier; he had had his tonsils taken out. His throat was a little sore, but he ate ice cream for weeks. He wasn't scared.

"When can we do it!" I screamed.

"Shush! Everyone's sleeping," she whispered, "and your father isn't feeling too well. Anyway, I have to make an appointment for this Dr. Kingsley to examine you, and he will decide whether or not surgery would help."

Big Lou, wearing his baggy plaid boxer shorts and sleeveless T-shirt, appeared in the kitchen doorway.

"What's all the screamin' about?" he whined and frowned like a little boy as he held his head with both hands.

"He knows," my mother simply responded.

"Hunh? Whu? Oh? Oh. Oh! Well, uh, ya' see, son, sometimes adults drink too much, and the next day—"

"No!" My mother covered her face with her hands. "About the operation!"

I picked up a back issue of *Life* magazine from one of the many end tables in the spacious dark waiting room of the Blue Island Medical Clinic. Every slight sound echoed off the tile floor and throughout the stale air. People whispered as if they were in a library. The dimly lit room housed huge drab paintings on the dull green walls. The darkly stained wooden furniture provided little comfort to the many patients who perused the curled pages of the dated magazines on the end tables or their own reading material. Some impatient patients displayed their displeasure of waiting by tapping their feet, sighing, and frowning. Others just closed their eyes and slept.

My mother had anticipated a long wait and brought along one of her many paperback novels. She had picked me up earlier from Park School so I could make a two o'clock appointment with Dr. Kingsley. It was now 3:40, and we still hadn't been called to see the doctor.

I invented a game to pass the time. It was a variation of the game that Mike, Dwayne, and I played—*Name That Car.* I titled this game *Name That Sickness* and shamelessly admit that I still play it as an adult. My mother thought the game was rude and refused to play, so I challenged myself. The object was to figure out what was wrong with the patients in the waiting room. Some with their bandaged eyes or noses, arms in slings, or legs in casts provided no challenge at all; most people, however, appeared quite normal and forced me to search for clues. A middle-aged red-haired woman occasionally reached beneath her long cotton dress and loudly scratched her thigh. I figured she had some kind of contagious rash that she generously passed onto the seat of her wooden chair. One old guy wearing rimless glasses and a double-breasted blue suit had me baffled until he sneezed six times straight onto the cover of his *Look* magazine. The cover of the *Life* magazine on my lap pictured actor Ralph Bellamy posing as FDR, a character he played in a movie. I imagined tiny sneeze germs crawling over Mr. Bellamy's face, and I carefully replaced the magazine onto the end table near me.

A swinging door flew open and a flash of bright light briefly illuminated the dark waiting room. A less-than-pretty young nurse dressed in her white uniform, white cap, and white winged glasses burst through the swinging door.

"Mr. Gren-Green-Green-burl-burg-Greenburg," she creatively misread from a large card.

The old guy slowly replaced his *Look* magazine and rose from his chair. He blessed our air four more times with sneezes before following the nurse through the swinging door.

Out of sheer boredom I picked up the potentially infectious *Life* magazine again and thumbed through it. A gruesome story featured a killing spree by a nineteen-year-old Nebraska boy and his fourteen-year-old girlfriend. After killing the girl's parents and her siblings, they killed eight more people before police captured them. I wondered as I stared at the picture of the young killer, Charles Starkweather, if people had made fun of him as a youngster. I wondered if his temper evolved like mine had and if those people might be alive if Charles could have developed a sense of humor to diffuse his temper.

A flash of white light interrupted my thoughts.

"Lou-Louise-Louis Ma-Mac-Maca—"

"That's us." My mother rescued the pitiful young nurse and motioned for me to follow her through the swinging door.

The nurse led us through the long fluorescent-lit corridor. The stale air of the waiting room clashed with the curiously fresh air in this hallway. The sterile scent of rubbing alcohol permeated the atmosphere. She stopped at one of the many doors, put a large card in the slot, and opened it.

"Have a seat in here. The doctor will be in soon," she lied.

A high cushioned examining table with white paper strapped over the cushions dominated the center space in this typically small sterile medical examining room. An anatomy poster of an eyeball, posters warning against eye diseases, and a calendar interrupted the brightness of the white enamel walls. A closed wooden cabinet hung on the wall over a metal counter supporting large glass jars of cotton balls, swabs, and tongue depressors. My mother and I sat on the lone two white enamel wooden chairs and waited twenty minutes for the doctor to arrive.

The door opened and Dr. Kingsley's presence instantly filled the tiny room. Unlike Dr. Daley and most doctors I had known, he didn't wear a white lab coat. His long-sleeved brown plaid sport shirt, brown dress pants, and brown penny loafers somehow clashed with his dark Middle Eastern features. His thick black hair, wide bushy moustache, and black-rimmed glasses nearly covered his olive-skinned face.

"You must be Louis," he said with a slight accent.

He startled me; he was the only doctor who had ever talked *to* me rather than *about* me to my mother.

"Yes, sir," I answered.

He patted the cushioned examining table and said, "Have a seat up here, Louis, take off your glasses, and let's have a look at your left eye."

He switched off the room light and flicked on his hand-held examining light. The familiar dot of light immediately probed my eye.

"How's school?" Dr. Kingsley asked as he moved the dot of light around my eyeball.

"Okay.".

"Got a girlfriend?"

"No," I answered and blushed.

"Is your teacher pretty?"

I just giggled; she was beautiful.

He switched on the room light and flicked off the instrument light. The room never went totally dark.

"Well, Louis, I think we can straighten out that eye so that you won't need these anymore," he said as he handed my glasses to me.

He finally acknowledged my mother's presence and asked her, "When is he through with school?"

"The second week of June," she answered.

"Hmm." He squinted at the wall-calendar and thought. "Louis, your mom and I are going to have a look at the schedule in my office. She'll be back in a few minutes, and you can go home." He led my mother out the door and closed it.

I pushed my chair beneath the calendar that hung near the metal counter. I stood on the chair and counted the days with my finger—eighty-five days, eighty-five days until the last day of school. I leaned across the metal counter, took the top off the jar of tongue depressors, reached inside the jar, and grabbed a handful. They looked like oversized wooden spoons that kids used for eating ice cream from a Dixie cup. I stuffed them into my pocket and waited for my mother to return.

Chapter 21

Darkness.

Thick black suffocating darkness.

I was fully awake, yet my eyes perceived only deep scary darkness. From it the image of Mr. Charleston groping desperately on his front lawn appeared. He looked at me with his fearful and painful eyes; then, he smiled and laughed at me. His image faded, and the image of my father's father appeared in his coffin. Although he seemed to be asleep, his eyes were wide open, and his face expressed a rigidly frozen thin smile.

Death...I am dead...or blind, I thought.

"Ahhhhhhhhh!" I screamed and sat up suddenly as my hands reached for my face.

"No, Louis, No!" the unfamiliar female voices quietly exclaimed, and hands grabbed my arms and forced me to recline. "You'll tear the bandages."

Bandages? Bandages...The Operation...My left eye...But both eyes are bandaged, I realized and tried to wrestle free and grab my eyes.

"I'm blind! I'm blind!"

"You're not blind, Louis. The doctor wants both eyes closed. If you open your right eye, your left eye will want to open, too, and it won't heal properly," a female voice tried to reason with me, but the panic had already set in and I struggled to sit up.

"Doctor! He's out of control!" another voice summoned.

"Louis, Louis," a young male voice faded in. "It's okay. Hold his arm steady."

Someone held my arm flat onto the bed. A cool cotton-like sensation touched the top of my forearm followed by a long pinch and the scent of rubbing alcohol. My body surrendered into total relaxation.

The darkness became my friend, and I drifted into a dreamless sleep.

Chapter 22

"How the hell are we going to know he's awake if his eyes are bandaged?" Big Lou's voice awoke me.

"We'll just watch him. He'll move or something," my mother's quivering voice answered. "Look, his hands are moving! Pudge? Pudgie? You okay? You are okay, I mean. The doctor said everything went well. Don't be afraid, those are just bandages on your eyes."

Her gentle hands touched my forearm and held it in place.

My father's rough calloused hands secured my other arm.

"How do you feel, son?" he asked in an almost foreign whispering voice.

No darkness this time.

I didn't need my eyes; my imagination saw them clearly. Big Lou wore his favorite short-sleeved summer sport shirt, horizontal gray stripes of varying thickness with an occasional red strip interrupting the pattern. The top button opened to a 'V' revealing his high-neck white undershirt. Mom wore her favorite green-and-white-striped cotton summer dress. She wore red lipstick and her hair pulled tightly back.

"Can I touch the bandages?"

After a long silence while they probably mimed a discussion, my mother said softly, "Okay, but be careful. Don't press on them or tear them loose."

Their hands released my arms.

My hands moved like they weighed twenty pounds toward my face. The thick soft gauze stopped my fingers well above my eyes. The rough wide surgical tape stretched from my cheeks, over the gauze and across the bridge of my nose.

Feeling the bandages relieved me.

I wasn't blind …I wasn't dead.

"We got this for you, against my better judgment," my mother said and put something into my palm.

As my fingers closed around its slender rough shape I immediately guessed, "A Cub Scout knife!"

I had wanted one ever since Dwayne showed his knife to Mike, Rick, and me. We spent hours playing *Jim Bowie,* a short-lived TV series which opened with Bowie throwing a knife seemingly fifty yards into a slender hardwood tree where the blade firmly stuck, and the handle vibrated and twanged gradually still.

"Just be careful with it," Big Lou warned, "or your mother'll open it and use it on me."

This would be the first of several "pity gifts." I didn't understand why anyone deserved a gift just because that person was temporarily lame…except out of pity. Although I didn't understand the concept, I readily embraced it.

"In a few days they'll take off the right bandage, and you can come home," my mother explained.

"How long before the other one comes off?" I asked.

After a long pause my father answered, "Not long. Hey, I'll let you guess who these guys are."

A short clap of two hands followed by a mischievous giggle signaled my grandfather's entrance. Ray's familiar voice followed, "Hey, Big Jim, you look tough with those patches over your eyes."

My face spread into a broad smile.

"Your grandpa and me thought you might be able to use this in here," Ray added and placed an object into my palm. It felt like a solid pack of cigarettes. Smooth metal trim framed a section of wiry mesh on the face of it. I ran my fingers carefully over the entire object and discovered two ridged disks embedded in the top. My finger pushed one disk; it clicked, moved freely and loud tinny rock and roll music came blaring from the little "cigarette pack."

"Wow! A transistor radio!"

"Yeah, well, use this so ya' don't wake up all eight floors of the hospital," Ray said. His big hands covered the radio and when he snapped something on its top the music stopped. Someone stuck a rubbery plug into my right ear, and the music blared throughout my skull.

The bandages over my eyes created a new world for me; it was a world that sparked and challenged my imagination. My fear of darkness vanished. Darkness provided a blank canvass that begged me to fill it with colors, images, and stories. I spent hours listening to loud and soft sounds segueing through each other. From the sounds I created pictures and movement. When the nurses gossiped as they bathed me and changed my bed, the hospital room became a sunny beach with beautiful girls in skimpy swimsuits fawning over me. The black-and-white TV in my room aired *The*

Roy Rogers Show. I pitied Mike watching on his black-and-white set at home because the TV in my head featured Roy and Trigger in bright rich colors with spangling jewels embedded on Roy's shirt and Trigger's saddle.

My last night in the hospital seemed unusually quiet and serene; this tranquility led me into deep introspection and reminiscence. I wondered what kind of difference the operation would make upon my life. Would I look different? Would I feel different? Would kids still make fun of me? Would I still be the class clown?

I reached to my left, groped the top of the small nightstand, and felt the textured handle of my Cub Scout knife. A small smooth diamond shape embedded in the handle bore a tiny wolf's head that I remembered from Dwayne's knife. Imagining the wolf's head made me think of death—*The Wolf Man*—Michael Landon—Death; that was it!

Death.

Death still terrified me. Nightmares of Mr. Charleston and my deceased grandfather often haunted me both day and night. I had conquered my temper with a sense of humor and my fear of darkness with a vivid imagination. Someday, somehow, I would conquer my fear of death, also…but how?

Chapter 23

The warm June sun baked the red top and black body of our '53 Nash, but the cool early summer breeze refreshed my face as the car accelerated down LaSalle Street toward home. My mother peered over the large red steering wheel and always drove as if a child were planning to jump in front of us at any moment. I sat on my knees and leaned out the window; my unpatched right eye stared at the kids as they played summer games on the sidewalk along LaSalle.

We crossed 142nd Street, a half block from our house on Glen Lane. Most of our neighbors and their kids stood outside as if either a celebrity or an ambulance were expected. As my mother parked the Nash in our spot along LaSalle, the people slowly approached our car. They were waiting to see me.

No, they were waiting to see my eye.

After jumping out of the car and slamming the door shut I turned and faced a collage of squinting faces. They looked at me the same way people had looked at me whenever I had taken my glasses off and exposed my crossed left eye. The patch disappointed them; it was as if they had paid to see the two-headed man at the carnival and were told that he was out to lunch. They turned from me like I had just

snapped a group picture and the need for staring at the camera lens and saying, "Che-e-e-se" had expired. The adults,
embarrassed by their morbid curiosity, approached my
mother and feigned concern for me. The kids were less subtle:

"So, did they pull your eyeball out and turn it?"

"Is your eye straight or still crooked?"

"What's it like to be in a hospital?"

"When they takin' the patch off so we can see it?"

I tried to answer their questions as dishonestly as pos-
sible. I told them that during the operation they dropped my
eyeball on the floor and they had to wash it because it was all
dusty. After the operation, the nurses had to walk around the
hospital naked because the doctors didn't want them spreading germs from their infectious nurse uniforms.

I had no answer for "When they takin' the patch
off...?"

My father worked that day, so our teenage neighbor,
Penny, babysat for Beth and Terri. When my mother and I
walked into the house two-year-old Terri ran up to me,
hugged me, and returned to her headless Betsy-Wetsy doll.
Beth said, "Hi," but never looked up from her *Betty and
Veronica* comic book as she sat on the living room couch;
obviously she was jealous of all the attention I had been
receiving.

"Pudgie! Pudgie!" Penny said, scurried toward me
and then gave me a hug. "I heard you took a liking to rock
and roll after someone gave you a transistor, so I thought you
might like this."

She grabbed a maroon and gray metal box by its clear
plastic handle from the dining room table, unsnapped the

metal lid latch, and showed me the contents. The box contained all of her old 45 rpm rock and roll records.

"Thanks, Penny. This is great!"

"It'd be even greater if you had your own record player and didn't have to use *my* record player now," said Beth, still not looking up from her comic book.

After supper Big Lou made me sit at the table a little while longer so that he and my mother could have a talk with me.

"Now," he began as he smothered his Salem cigarette in some wet part of his plate, "the doctor gave us some ground rules for you, and I don't think you're gonna' like them. First, no strenuous, that means wild, activity like running around, playing baseball, for a while. No swimming and only two hours of TV a day."

"I figured all that, but what about when the patch comes off?"

My mother stood up and started clearing the table, and the annoying clatter of dishes and silverware hitting the kitchen sink began.

Big Lou gave her a look of annoyance and continued, "Well, when the patch comes off you can go back to doing your usual crazy things."

"Great, when's that gonna' be?"

The clatter of dishes and silverware stopped. My mother turned from the sink and gave me a serious look. My father's face froze in a wide-eyed expression. Finally, after several seconds of awkward silence, he said, "Probably not until about a week before school starts."

A sinking feeling overcame me and emptiness followed. That was all summer, I thought. Summer had just started. Tears began to gather beneath the patch and within my right eye.

"One more thing," he continued. "We're to see that you don't get too upset. Tears can retard, that means slow down, the healing process and be painful to your left eye."

That's like telling a guy with a bad heart that the slightest shocking news could upset and kill him. Big Lou was right about the tears. Beneath the patch, my eye burned from the hot salty fluid.

Mike, Rick, and Dwayne came around to see me several times over the next few days. My inactivity gradually bored them, however, and they stopped coming.

I couldn't blame them.

My baseball buddies (Jentz, Loll, Pews, and Smitty) came by once.

Gradually, within a few weeks, I was sinking into a deep dark depression. My energy level dwindled. My appetite decreased, and my weight dropped. All I wanted to do was to lie on my bed and stare at the ceiling with my exposed right eye.

* * *

Wednesday, 11:17 a.m.

"When did Paul (Wayne's cousin) write a letter to us (the Romans, Terri's married name)?" Kristin, my older niece, asks Terri.

The limo driver shuts the door, and Beth, Wayne, Terri, Bob, my two nieces, Dorinda and I settle in for the slow five-mile ride to the cemetery.

"What?" Terri counter-asks.

"The minister said, "...in Paul's letter to the Romans...""

"Oh my God!" Terri gasps. "I knew we pulled our kids out of Sunday school too soon!"

As if on cue, we erupt so that it sounds like one harmonious family laugh. We release all of the tension and depression that has mounted over the last four days.

While the limo lumbers along, however, we sink back into our private thoughts and somber moods. When we are within a block of the cemetery gates, the gloom returns.

The limo driver slams on the brakes, and we tumble toward the front. At the stoplight on 127th and Halsted Street, the driver of a beautiful baby blue and white classic antique 1958 Corvette convertible fails to yield the right-of-way to the funeral procession. The car speeds northbound down Halsted Street.

Through the tinted side window of the limo, my eyes follow its journey toward downtown Chicago; it becomes smaller, just a blue dot, then vanishes.

My depression vanishes, also.

* * *

My mother sensed my depression and sent me to stay with my grandparents in Harvey for a few days. Under most circumstances that would have been the right thing to do because usually my grandfather could cheer me up. His young heartedness and a devious sense of humor challenged my depression. He organized his neighborhood cronies, and they planned some boyish pranks to play on their younger adult neighbors. They told one of their victims that a huge raccoon had climbed down his chimney. When the guy climbed onto his roof to investigate, they took his ladder away and retreated to their respective houses. The wife of another young neighbor interrupted her husband mowing their lawn with their brand new Sears gas-powered lawnmower and called him to the phone. My grandfather kept him busy on the phone while his prankster cronies extracted the sparkplug from the mower. The poor guy sweated in the hot sun as he tried over and over again to start his shiny new mower with the clean white rope-pull starter. One by one, my grandfather and his friends emerged from their homes; each man sipped from a cold can of beer and offered useless advice for starting it.

But even Grandpa's antics weren't amusing me. After dinner they sat me in front of the TV to watch one of those sadistic Walt Disney movies. I could feel my eyes well as I watched Dumbo's mother locked in chains in a bar-windowed small cell and unable to get to her crying big-eared baby elephant. My sorrow turned to anger when my forbidden tears burned and stung my left eye.

Just about that time, Ray walked into the house. He occasionally dropped by my grandparents' after work just for a visit. When he saw me he immediately sensed that something was wrong. My grandmother described my depressed state as "the blues."

Ray said, "C'mon, let's go for a ride."

My grandmother stuttered as she tried to come up with an excuse for me to stay. By now, everyone liked Ray, but they also knew he had a wild streak in him.

"We'll just get some ice cream," he said, and that seemed to satisfy her.

I got into the car, but even the thought of ice cream and the '57 Chevy didn't cheer me. Ray was talking about how skinny he was as a kid. His mother thought he had TB and took him to the doctor. Finally, they discovered that he had a tapeworm.

I didn't pay much attention to his story, but I started wondering where we were going. The far southwest suburbs of Chicago, later known as Orland Park and Frankfort, were rural back then. The area consisted mostly of cornfields and country roads, and Ray seemed familiar with all of it.

Finally, he stopped the Chevy on a gravel/dirt road surrounded by cornfields. He pressed the brake pedal to the floor with his left foot. Then, gradually he pressed his other foot on the accelerator. The 283 engine cried and screamed as if angered by the inhibiting brakes. He released the brake pedal, and the back wheels spun, spitting crackling gravel behind us. Ray said, "Hang on," and the tires grabbed the road; within seconds we traveled at eighty miles an hour. We made hairpin turns, slowing just enough to see that the green blur around us was actually tall cornstalks.

Ray smiled and cackled, and I did the same. This ride was frighteningly more fun than any rollercoaster ride. As if he saw a wall in front of him, Ray came to a stop that spun the car to a ninety- degree angle with the road. Darkness had replaced the twilight, but the headlights illuminated the tall cornstalks ahead of us.

"Don't say a word!" Ray commanded, and in a moment there was almost complete silence, then the growing distant whining of a siren.

"Shit!" he whispered. He shut off the lights and gunned the Chevy off the road and into the cornfield. About twenty yards into the field he stopped and turned the engine off. We looked through the rear window into total darkness. As the siren whined louder and louder the road became vaguely more visible as the flickering red and white spinning light illuminated it. My chest pounded with each flicker of the light.

Then, the siren and the flashing light were gone. Ray produced a high-pitched giggle, and I joined in.

The vehicle hadn't been a squad car, but an ambulance.

He backed the Chevy onto the road and sped back to civilization. We talked and laughed about the adventure all the way to the first stoplight. As we waited for it to change, Ray said, "I guess we better cover our asses and come back with some ice cream."

We stopped at the Dairy Queen on Ridge Road in the suburb of Homewood, an affluent suburb southeast of Harvey. We got a pint of vanilla for my grandparents. I don't remember what Ray got, but I got a large vanilla cone dipped in melted chocolate.

As we pulled up to my grandparents' house on Lexington Avenue I didn't know what to say. All of my depression had disappeared somewhere in those dense cornfields. I no longer envied my friends for the summer fun that they were having. I pitied them for what they had just missed.

Ray spoke for me, "Listen, as far as Grandma knows, we just went for ice cream. Right?"

"Right."

"Now, get your ass outa'here before you get chocolate on my upholstery, and I have to kick it…your ass that is."

I smiled, slid out the car, and slammed the door shut.

Through the opened window I said, "Thanks, Ray."

He just nodded and wisely drove slowly and quietly from the curb.

Chapter 24

The surgical tape pulled at my skin as Dr. Kingsley ripped the eye patch from my face. My eyelid remained closed despite my efforts to open it, so the doctor gently bathed it with a warm wet gauze pad. Gradually, my left lid opened, but the eye saw only blurred fuzzy colorless images. Dr. Kingsley deposited drops of a heavy liquid from an eye-dropper into my eye. I blinked several times; with each blink the world became clearer and more colorful, until finally my left eye perceived everything as clearly as the right.

"Your mother may have to do this every morning for a few weeks, Louis," the doctor explained, "but eventually your eye will open and see clearly on its own. Now let's take a closer look."

He inspected the eye like an artist admiring his unveiled masterpiece. He clicked on his hand-held probing light and directed the dot around my left eye, then clicked it off and sat back for a more distant view of his work. A broad smile that defied his modest nature bloomed on his face as he placed a small rectangular mirror into my palm.

"Take a look for yourself, Louis."

Astonishment.

It wasn't straightness and correctness of my left eye that produced the astonishment. My talented imagination had seen this perfect eye many times. My reflection sans glasses produced it. My glasses always hung on my face whenever I saw my reflection; somehow the lenses gave the illusion that my eye was straight.

My return from the hospital months earlier had prepared me for the freak show that followed. People stared shamelessly into my left eye as if they were peaking through a keyhole. The sight of a normal straight eye somewhat disappointed them, however, and they soon regarded me with the same anonymity as everyone else. Kids at school paid very little attention to my new look.

School started as usual on the day after Labor Day. During that short week the school district routinely administered achievement tests. While the class struggled with the math portion of the test, the school secretary, followed by a tall lanky boy wearing a plaid short-sleeved sport shirt and cuffed blue jeans, brushed by my desk. The secretary whispered to Miss Lupo, our second-grade teacher, then left the classroom.

"Class, I'm sorry to disturb you," Miss Lupo interrupted, "but we have a new student who I want you all to meet. His name is—"

She gave the boy a friendly quizzical look.

"Tommy," he responded weakly, "Tommy Burnside."

"Tommy Burnside!" she repeated as if she knew all along. "Now go back to your testing while I get Tommy settled in here."

He occupied a seat in the front of the class. He began filling out the information section of his test. His tall figure and brush-cut hair style revealed that he had huge white ears. Pues, who sat behind me, nudged me with his pencil and whispered, "Hey, get a load of Dumbo!"

Several students around us heard the comment and snickered; I joined them. Tommy's white ears grew red. My entire face reddened, and I stopped snickering. For years I had been on Tommy's side of the snickering. Less than a week had passed since Dr. Kingsley unveiled my corrected left eye, and already I had joined the cruel ridiculing masses.

Later, at recess, I asked Tommy to join a bunch of us playing kickball. During the game, he not only fielded the ball, but several comments about his ears, also. He didn't say or do anything, but his reddened face clearly showed that he was angry, embarrassed, or both.

Miss Lupo blew her stainless steel whistle, and we lazily walked back to the school building. I caught up with Tommy.

"Hey, listen," I began. "Don't pay any attention to them."

He pretended as if he hadn't heard me.

"Just smile and make some kind of joke. They'll leave ya' alone."

"How would you know?" he asked and looked down at me with squinting eyes.

"I just know."

Our almost-life-size-barely-three-dimensional-tin cop guided us across Wentworth Avenue at the front of the school building when school ended at three-thirty. It must have been too expensive to hire a real cop during the 1950s because most school districts employed these tin cops. The smiling figure held a white-gloved hand in the air while his other hand held a sign reading *Slow, School Zone*. Our tin cop provided a canvas for an artistic kid who blackened out the cop's teeth and drew genitals on him. Wentworth was a pot-holed rocky dirt road that naturally slowed cars down without the help of a toothless indecently exposed tin cop.

Steve Baylog (Jentz nicknamed him *Baytwig*) was the only kid in my class who walked in my direction, north on Wentworth. Steve was a chunky kid with stiff brown hair sticking straight up into a crew-cut.

On this day, Tommy walked with us.

"You live around here, Tommy?" I asked

He extended his long lanky arm and pointed down Wentworth toward where it curved into 141st Street.

"I live around the corner down there on 141st."

"Yeah? I live on the other side of these garages on Glen Lane, and Steve here lives on LaSalle just next to Glen Lane."

We stopped to part company at the end of the long garage building.

"See you guys tomorrow." Tommy nodded.

"Yeah, see ya' tomorrow," I said.

Steve couldn't resist being the asshole that he was.

"Hey, Tommy," he quipped, "can you git radio signals on those ears?"

Tommy sucked in his lower lip and got crimson.

I elbowed him and gave him a remember-what-I-told-ya' look.

Tommy exhaled and gave me a long thoughtful stare. Then, he held his hands up to his ears, moved his hands in and out like his hands and ears were repelling poles of magnets and said, "woo, woo, woo," mimicking receiving radio waves.

All three of us cracked up.

"You're okay, Tommy," Steve said and nodded. "You're okay."

"Later." Tommy pointed at us and continued down Wentworth.

Steve and I turned into the alley behind the garages

What happened next scared me as much as it must have scared Steve. I grabbed him by his collar and forced him down into the weeds and bushes between the alley and the garage building. When he was flat on his big stomach, I sat with my knees on his back, grabbed a handful of his stiff crew-cut, and turned his head to the side. I could feel him trembling beneath me.

"Whatsa' matter with you!" Steve squealed.

I reached into my pocket, pulled out my Cub Scout knife, skillfully opened the blade with one hand, and held it to his lips.

"You ever make fun of him again, I'm gonna' cut that fuckin' smile right off your face," I whispered close to his exposed ear. (I didn't even know what *fuckin'* meant. I had heard some neighborhood teenagers use the word when they got mad or wanted to act tough; then, they'd guiltily look around to see if any adults had heard. I knew, therefore, that the word was both powerful and forbidden.)

I let him up, and he glared at me like he had just escaped the grasp of a wild beast.

"You're nuts!" he said, then turned down the alley, and ran toward LaSalle Street.

Across Wentworth a vacant lot with high weeds stretched from Park School all the way to 141st Street. A grayish brown rabbit sat on the edge of the lot just off the gravel/dirt road. The rabbit was barely visible against the tall brown weeds of the prairie; however, I could feel the cold stare from its unblinking doll-like black eye as it watched me from the other side of the road. I wondered if it had witnessed my attack on Steve. Its motionless body and dead stare gave no clues.

I scanned my surroundings for a rock to throw in its direction and scare it away, but when I looked up again…it was gone. Clumps of weeds bent deeper and deeper within the lot as the rabbit scampered home.

I closed my Cub Scout pocketknife, returned it to my pocket, and did the same.

Chapter 25

I had just stepped into our house after school on this bitter cold first day of December when the phone rang. No one seemed to be home, so I answered it.

"You gotta' come over and see what my dad brought home!" Mike said.

"Okay, okay, calm down!"

He must have dragged Rick right from their classroom after school because both of them answered my knocking on the back door. They ushered me to the basement. The stairwell echoed Bobby Darin's voice singing, "Splish splash I was takin' a bath, all upon a Saturday night…"

Colored lights rainbowed around the face of the machine, changing colors as the music played. The jukebox's pulsating rock beat and alternating colors mesmerized us; it was like a giant carnival compacted into one large furniture piece. All of the songs were rock and roll or pop songs that were only a year or two old.

"Dad got it today from one of his restaurant owner friends," Mike explained. "See how the front opens? If you stick your finger through here you can hit the selector switch and play as many records as you want without payin'. But ya' gotta' be careful when ya' touch stuff back here cuz my dad says ya' could get a big electric shock."

This sounded like a challenge to daredevil Rick, so he wet his fingers and felt around the inside wiring until he finally got a shock that nearly lit him up like the colors on the door.

* * *

Wednesday, 12:10 p.m.

After the gravesite service, the limo driver drops us off at our cars parked in the funeral home lot. We briefly discuss directions to the restaurant where we had planned a luncheon for the mourners.

I jump into the driver's seat of my white Ford pick-up, and Dorinda hops into the passenger's seat. Almost before we hear the engine turn over, I turn on the radio. Jerry Lee Lewis's voice resonates from the speakers and fills the cab:

You shake my nerves and you rattle my brain
Too much of love drives a man insane
You broke my will, but a thrill
Goodness gracious great balls of fire!

"Don't you listen to anything but 'oldies'?" Dorinda complains.

"The oldies make me feel good."

* * *

While we listened to *The Purple People Eater* I reminisced about the time I had spent lying in the hospital and listening to rock and roll on my little transistor. After leaving the hospital, I listened to the radio less and less—partly because of my depression and partly because the Chicago radio stations stopped playing rock and roll for a while. A

local religious leader, Cardinal Stritch of Chicago's archdio-
cese, demanded that radio stations ban the playing of rock
and roll and ordered Catholics to boycott stations that played
it. After my wild ride with Ray, I explored the metal box of
records that Penny had given me. I pulled out each 45 rpm
record, read the label, and played it on Beth's little alligator
suitcase-model record player. That metal record box became
a treasure chest of rock and roll. I closed my eyes and
absorbed the harmony of the Everly Brothers, the rockabilly
style of Johnny Cash and Carl Perkins, and, most notably, the
unique Buddy Holly sound. My favorites included Holly's
That'll be the Day and Paul Anka's *Diana*. My hands emulated what I thought the drummer was doing whenever I listened to a rock and roll song. I felt a warm flame kindling my
desire to take drum lessons again.

I had spent the pleasant cool Indian summer days of
September and October either indoors listening to records or
outdoors playing sports with my baseball buddies. The cold
winds and rain of November, however, forced us indoors
where we became restless.

One November Saturday afternoon we explored the
new *Ben Franklin Five-and-Dime Store* on 144th Street. The
sporting goods aisle immediately attracted Loll and Jentz
where they inspected cheap sawdust baseballs and rubber
footballs. Pues spent his time and money in the board game
and book sections. Smitty focused on his plan to shoplift a
clear plastic bag of cats-eye marbles; he paced the toy department aisle like an alley cat watching for mice. As soon as I
entered the store a set of topless shoeboxes atop the checkout
counter attracted my scanning eyes. Behind the shoeboxes a

cardboard sign read "Used Jukebox 45's—39 cents each."
The people in the checkout line half-circled me as I patiently
thumbed through the titles. I picked out a forgettable Tommy
Sands record, *Teenage Crush,* and Elvis's *Teddy Bear.* Mean-
while, Smitty breezed past me and hustled out the door; he
successfully pulled off his big marble bag heist. As I stood in
the checkout line with my two 45's and a dollar in my hand, I
wondered if I would have to fight with Beth over the use of
her record player when I got home.

The drum roll introduction to Buddy Holly's *Peggy
Sue* boomed from the jukebox speaker and awakened me
from my *Ben Franklin* daydream. Mike and Rick were setting the tracks for Mike's electric train set on the basement
floor.

A record player! That was it! That's what I would
request for a Christmas present. But it was already December
1st; I had to request it before my parents finished their Christmas shopping.

"I gotta' go, guys," I said as I grabbed my jacket and
ran up the basement stairs. "I'll be late for supper."

"It's only 4:30!" Mike countered.

I didn't even feel the bitter cold through my thin
jacket as I jogged across the alley toward our back door.

When I opened the door the familiar sounds coming
from the TV speaker signaled that people were home. As I
burst into the living room, however, I knew that this was not
the time to request a Christmas present.

Beth and Terri huddled around my mother on the sofa
as she held them closely under her arms. Tears streamed
down my mother's face as she stared at the TV screen.

Chapter 26

A horror movie…but it wasn't a horror movie; it was live coverage during the 4:30 WGN-TV news broadcast. Rich black smoke billowed from the second floor windows of a school building as the high-pitched screams of children echoed inside and then out the broken windows into the bitter December air. Parents outside the building shrieked with terror as they pressed against the police barricades. A blazing fire had erupted at Our Lady of Angels School on Chicago's west side just minutes before the 1,500 children would have been dismissed for the day. The fire was out of control.

I sat on the sofa next to Terri. She squirmed from beneath my mother's arm and buried her face in my lap just to avoid watching the horrifying news coverage. A father screamed, "Jump, son, jump!" when he recognized his son leaning out a second-story window, but the boy just cried helplessly as the black smoke and broad shooting flames swallowed him back into the building.

Big Lou stood silently behind the sofa. Normally the rattling of the thermos inside his black metal lunch pail signaled his arrival at around five o'clock. But today he seemed to appear as an apparition. He wore his faded blue denim work cap and his old gray winter coat and carried his lunch pail loosely in his hand. He shook his head in disbelief, his eyes transfixed on the TV screen. The wild animal stirred inside him, and he didn't know how to control it. After putting his lunch pail away and hanging up his coat, he sat at the kitchen table with his head in his hands.

We ate dinner in silence—no traditional "How was school today?" or small talk. My father had a way of making Beth and me feel ashamed of our existence—especially when he was depressed from fighting that wild animal inside him. Terri was too young to perceive his dark moods.

After supper he lit his ritualistic after-dinner cigarette and took a long deep drag. The exhaled smoke provided a thin shield between us and him. He put his elbows onto the table and leaned into the gray smoke.

"You kids don't know how lucky you are." At first he seemed to be talking to himself. Then, as the smoke cleared, he eyed each of us as if we had committed a crime and needed to confess. "Parents, a roof over your head, food on the table…those kids have nothing …they're gone."

We lowered our heads and kept quiet.

"Expect a little less for Christmas," he continued. "We're sending money to the school and the families of those kids who died."

Beth and I felt bad enough about the kids who died. Now we had to feel guilty because we were alive.

The following evening, dinner returned to its less somber and more traditional practices. Big Lou lit his cigarette and asked, "How was school?"

Beth and I provided our dull it-was-okay answers and waited for our equally dull dessert, Cherry Jell-O. He set his Salem cigarette on an ashtray and opened the *Chicago Daily*

News to the sports page over the clattering of dishes as Mom cleared the table.

The front page curled toward my face as my father read. A class picture much like class pictures taken at our Park School covered half the front page. I scanned the photos. The children smiled behind shined and bespectacled faces just like my schoolmates. My scanning fixated on one photograph—Mary, the black-haired little girl who had handed me my glasses after my fight two years earlier. I hadn't seen her since we were in a park district *Learn to Swim* program the summer before second grade. She announced then that her family was moving and she would be attending a new school in the fall. The headline over the picture read: *Fatalities of Our Lady Fire*.

My body and mind protected me from something; I had no feelings, just numbness. Mom, Dad, Beth, and even little Terri stared at me as if my eye had gone crooked again.

"Are you okay?" Big Lou asked.

"Yes," I answered, "may I be excused?"

He nodded, and I quietly stood up, walked into the bathroom, locked the door behind me, sat on the edge of the bathtub, and waited...waited for some kind of feeling or thought, but nothing came. Then, from somewhere deep within me, that untamed animal grew. It shook and possessed me. There was no stopping it, and I screamed, cried, and dove at the toilet bowl where I vomited my dinner in one painful heave.

Chapter 27

I feared sleeping, feared dreaming, so I sat up in my bed all night. I recognized and respected the pattern that had developed in my life—death, guilt, then horrible nightmares. The soft light from the streetlamp on Glen Lane seeped through the window of my attic bedroom and blended with the rich darkness. The mixture of darkness and soft light produced a shadowless gray box against the wall. That grayness and the distant clackety-clack of trains passing along the track by the Wentworth prairie kept me awake and safe throughout the night.

The next morning in school, Miss Lupo confirmed that the rumor was true; Mary had perished in the fire. She announced that a collection would be taken throughout the week and sent along with a card from Park School to her family. Mrs. Bennett thought that Park School students might need some counseling concerning Mary's death and perhaps death itself. In the 1950s most public grammar schools in the Chicago area didn't hire counselors or school psychologists; therefore, she sent the district school nurse from Roosevelt School.

Although this nurse didn't provide us with much comfort or insight about the nature of death, she did provide us with some needed comic relief. She was so bundled up that we could hardly see her face when she limped into our classroom. She placed her huge shiny black purse directly in front of Miss Lupo's face on the teacher's desk, took off her heavy long woolen black winter coat and huge knit floppy hat, and revealed that she had the figure of Olive Oil and the face of Popeye. She pulled a large wooden chair to the front of the room, sat down, and lit a Winston cigarette. After taking a long drag from the Winston and coughing out a throatful of smoke, her gravelly Popeye's voice, asked, "You kids got any questions?"

After a long silence, Jentz raised his hand and asked her if she kept a can of spinach in her purse.

Sleep overtook me that night, and just as I had feared, my death nightmare returned. It started as usual with Mr. Charleston staring at me with pain and fear in his eyes. His face dissolved into the image of my grandfather lying in his coffin. His mouth widened into a thin smile, and his eyes opened to a cold penetrating stare. His image dissolved, and I stood alone in the playground at Park School. It was dark, and a cool whistling wind blew steadily in my face; the faint shadow of the school building appeared in the darkness. "Here, Louis, I think these are yours," Mary's soft voice echoed from her faintly glowing ghost beside me. She held a pair of yellow-rimmed glasses without lenses in her delicate white hand. She wore a frilly white gown more appropriate for a full-grown woman. Her green eyes sparkled and her wavy black hair gently blew in the cool wind, but only momentarily. Her sparkling green eyes turned a bright hot red, and her black wavy hair turned to thick black billowing smoke. She opened her mouth, and an ear-piercing shriek echoed throughout the playground. I held my ears and tried to drown the shrieking with my own screams.

I awoke in a sitting position with my hands over my ears; the hall light went on, and Beth ran down the stairs yelling, "Mom! Mom!"

Within a minute, footsteps scurried up the stairs. My mother and Beth stood as silhouettes in the doorway of my room.

"Pudgie, what's wrong?" my mother asked.

"Just a bad dream."

She ordered Beth back to bed, and then asked, "What were you dreaming about?"

I never shared my nightmares or my dreams with my parents. Perhaps I thought they would think I was crazy or effeminate; or perhaps I just wanted to keep my dreams personal. Maybe it was all of the above.

"I don't know. It was just a scary dream."

"Do you want to sleep downstairs tonight?"

When Beth and I were younger, we occasionally slept with our parents (despite Big Lou's protests) if we had awakened from a nightmare. I was older and too proud for that, but I didn't want to be left alone either.

"Can I just sleep on the couch downstairs?"

"Sure."

I gathered my pillow and blankets. My mother walked me downstairs with her hand on my shoulder. I quickly made a makeshift bed with my blankets and pillow, and my mother tucked me in. She kissed me on the forehead and said, "Sweet dreams."

The coolness of the pillow and the warmth of the blankets made me feel safe. Big Lou's loud rhythmic snoring resonated from the nearby bedroom. Ironically, the snoring sounded like a lullaby to me, and I drifted into a deep dreamless sleep.

The nightmares continued three or four nights a week over the next several weeks. I didn't wake up screaming anymore; I was less afraid and more annoyed by them. They disrupted my sleep at night and my concentration during the day.

The excitement of Christmas was everywhere. Colorful decorations lit up the neighborhood and downtown streets. Christmas music blared from the storefronts, radios, and television sets. Nature decorated the evergreens with light snow showers.

Christmas was my favorite time of year, but this year my nightmares and daydreams of death left me numb. I envied Terri's childish Christmas spirit: her belief in Santa, her glazed eyes at the sight of our decorated tree, and her commitment to learn every carol that she heard. On Christmas morning she began a tradition that continued throughout her childhood. At dawn she stood at the bottom of the stairs that led to Beth's and my attic bedrooms and yelled, "You guys? You guys, get up so we can open our presents!" Even if Beth and I were wide awake, we feigned deep sleep until she shook our beds and made us get up.

Our parents neatly stacked the presents under the tree in three separate piles. My father had spoken the truth; the piles were shorter than usual because we had donated money to the families of the children who died in the Our Lady of Angels fire. Nevertheless, Santa had been generous. Some families in our neighborhood observed the orderly custom of one person at a time opening presents so everyone could see each gift and share in the joy. At our house we just dove at our piles and ripped off the wrapping paper. The paper rose from the floor like bubble bath suds from an overflowing bathtub. Occasionally from the depths of the rising paper someone would say, "Thank you, Santa!"

I tried to get into the Christmas spirit, but my heart wasn't in it. I manufactured a smile and approached my gifts. My pile consisted of four gifts. Some uninspired wrapping told me that three gifts were a baseball bat, a baseball, and a record album. I started with the mysterious fourth gift; it was about the size of a briefcase and moderately heavy.

I tore off the cheap red-green wrapping paper; my manufactured smile turned real. It was a record player, just like Beth's except for two important distinctions: One, hers was alligator red, and mine was alligator green; two, hers was hers, and mine was mine.

The large colored electric lights from the tree reflected off the shiny alligator- green cover and the delicate glittering tree ornaments. A sweet syrupy scent from the long Scotch pine tree needles spiced the air. Perry Como sang *O Little Town of Bethlehem* from the record album playing on the hi-fi console.

It was Christmas morning.

Chapter 28

I had had neither daydreams nor nightmares about death in over a month. Since Christmas morning, each day got better and better. The January snow showers turned Riverdale into a winter amusement park for kids. Winters in Chicago could be brutal for adults; they had to drive on the icy roads, shovel snow off roofs, etc. For kids, however, a winter storm meant no school, money for shoveling snow, snow forts, snowball fights, and sledding.

During the early morning hours of February 3rd, snow fell and continued to fall throughout the day. A rumor started that we'd be sent home early from school and Park School would be closed the next day. Although the rumor proved to be false, speculating about school cancellation was fun. Mike and I hurried home and changed into clothes that would soon be soaked from our determination to build a snow fort.

After we had spent about an hour rolling snow into child-size balls for our fort walls, our mothers called us for supper. We knew we'd catch hell for getting our clothes all wet, but building a beautiful snow fort was well worth it.

* * *

Wednesday, 12:28 p.m.

People who had traveled straight from the cemetery to the restaurant had a very short trip; therefore, the lot is packed when we arrive. I park on a side street.

Just before I turn off the radio, Buddy Holly's *That'll Be the Day* blasts from the speakers.

I begin to sweat.

* * *

I changed clothes and sat on the living room floor while my father reclined in "his chair," read *The Chicago Daily News,* and listened to the TV newscast. The news generally bored me, but one news story snagged my attention. Fahey Flynn, the newscaster, delivered it with an enlarged photograph behind him. Buddy Holly with his boyish grin, black-rimmed glasses, and curly jet-black hair appeared in the photograph; his singles, including *That'll Be the Day, Maybe Baby,* and *Peggy Sue*, blasted from the speaker of my record player nearly every day.

"Three young rock and roll singers were tragically killed in a plane crash early this morning. Buddy Holly, Ritchie Valens, and J.P. Richardson, better known as 'The Big Bopper,' died when their chartered airplane crashed in a cornfield shortly after takeoff in Clearwater, Iowa."

As Fahey continued, film footage of the plane wreckage appeared; I turned away…but I couldn't escape the horror. As my father read the inside pages of the newspaper, the front page headline screamed, ROCKERS KILLED. An enlarged photo covered about half of the front page and detailed the plane wreckage including body parts. I closed my eyes, but I could still see the twisted metal and the dead bodies in my head.

I wouldn't eat dinner and wouldn't say what was wrong. My mother thought I was getting sick but withheld her sympathy since she had warned me that playing in the cold outdoors while wearing wet clothes and not wearing a hat would lead to sickness. She ordered me to go directly to bed.

In my dark attic bedroom, I lay awake with the dim light from my tabletop radio near the head of my bed. WLS was broadcasting a tribute to Buddy Holly, Ritchie Valens, and the Big Bopper.

I turned down the volume so low that only my ears heard Buddy Holly's lyrics:

That'll be the day, hey, hey…when I die.

Chapter 29

My nightmares returned that night. Mr. Charleston, my grandfather, Mary, burning school buildings, screaming children, Buddy Holly, plane crashes—they polluted my dreams at night and preoccupied my thoughts during the day.

Wednesday morning I dressed for school, ate breakfast, said, "Good-bye," walked to school, and sat at my desk. I existed; I functioned; that was it. Nothing made sense anymore. Why laugh at Smitty's art project, a drawing of a witch with the teacher's name under it? Smitty or Miss Lupo could be dead by the end of the day. Why listen to the rock and roll music on the record player? The artists may just die and depress me. Why waste time learning about history in school if we're going to be worm food just like the people in our history book? Those thoughts left me numb…but numbness was better than sadness, pain, or fear.

By Saturday morning I felt totally withdrawn from the world. Whenever my mother suspected something wrong with Beth, Terri, or me, she stuck a thermometer in our mouths. Apparently my problem was more than mental; I had a fever of 101. She had a problem, too. Mom had invited friends and relatives to an open house on Sunday to celebrate Terri's and my birthdays.

"Oh my God! What am I gonna' do? I've invited all these people to come tomorrow. Now I have to call and cancel. I don't even know who all I invited! Oh my God!"

Big Lou watched like a psychiatrist waiting for his patient to vent. He knew the routine: She'll pace around, rant, and rave; then, she'll sit at the kitchen table, put her head in her hands, cry, or not, and listen to him.

He sat across from her.

"Look," he began as he lit a Salem, "why don't you talk to Dr. Gaetano first. It may be nothing. Maybe I'll just have to drive him to Hazel Crest for a penicillin shot, and he'll be fine."

Dr. Gaetano was the family doctor, not just for the immediate family, but for my father's brothers, sisters, their families, and my mother's side of the family, too. To the adults, he was something of a wizard. He made house calls; he diagnosed and prescribed over the phone, without expensive tests—and people got well! To kids, he was just a bald guy who gave painful shots in the ass and gagging liquid medicines.

After speaking with the doctor on the phone, Mom sighed away her anxieties and spoke. "Well, he said it's just a virus going around. We should put him upstairs to bed, keep him away from the company, and give him aspirin and a prescription that he'll call in to Vern at Evans' Drugs. He should be well enough to go to school on Monday."

Great, I thought, not only will I miss my own party, but I *won't* miss school. I lay in bed all day Saturday staring at the knotty pine walls of my tiny bedroom. Everyone was comfortable with my illness because Dr. Gataeno said it was physical, not mental or emotional. People in my

neighborhood during the 1950s didn't have mental or emotional illnesses. "Something they ate," the weather, or "it's
going around" explained away those types of illnesses, and
the "Dr. Gaetanos" perpetuated the process. My nightmares
were "just the aspirin working" or "the fever raging." My
depression would disappear with the fever or wash away with
my grandmother's homemade soup.

I knew better. The physical symptoms resulted from
nearly a week of sleepless nights and days with barely enough
appetite to keep my body nourished.

The Saturday afternoon sun beamed through my window and lit up the room. As I lay in my small built-in-the-
wall bunk, I felt like a part of my bedroom clutter: the books
I never read in the built-in bookcase, the built-in desk with
pencils and a spiral notebook strewn carelessly on top, the
Cubs pennant thumbtacked on the knotty pine wall, the alli-
gator-green record player on the TV table with the overstuffed
metal record box below it, the nightstand with the gaudy pink
tabletop radio that used to be in our kitchen, and me.

Boredom bred a dangerous fear—fear of self. I began
to fear my own thoughts. The more I thought about death, the
more I fed my nightmares, which led to more thinking during
the day about people dying, which led to more nightmares.
This thought pattern started as a single cycle but evolved into
a downward spiral leading me into a suffocating unfamiliar
darkness; however, with the aid of aspirin and the prescribed
medicine that my mother forced down me, I surrendered to a
deep dreamless sleep Saturday night.

My fever broke Sunday morning. My pajamas and
sheets were soaked with sweat. After taking a bath and

changing into clean pajamas, I went back to bed and felt much better. I tried to convince my parents that I was well and therefore able to join the party later. They remained unconvinced. I lay in bed all day, thus allowing the boredom to nourish my fears again.

Throughout the afternoon muffled conversation and laughter seeped through the floorboards of my room as people came for cake, drinks, and jokes and left. The late afternoon winter darkness heightened my loneliness and boredom, and my bedroom became a chamber of horrors and depression. The nightmares that terrified me in my sleep now appeared like a 3-D horror movie while I was awake. I closed my eyes and covered my ears, but the movie continued on my eyelids and inside my head; it was a moving collage of fire, shrieking figures including Mary, Mr. Charleston, Beth, Terri, Mike, and even me. I dared not scream and alert the houseful of people to my pathetic state. I sat up and the horror movie stopped abruptly. My body steamed with sweat. I moved toward the large window over the window seat. My father had constructed a storm window; I flipped loose the eye hooks that held it in place, and it easily popped out the frame. A set of French door-like windows opened to the outside. I grabbed the cold metal latches at the center and pulled them away from the center metal strip that divided the opening in half. With one strong push I forced the windows open, and the fresh cold winter air rushed through my warm trembling body and inside the room; it revived and refreshed me. The ground looked like white icing on a Danish pastry, oval patches of brown grass randomly peeked through the thin layer of snow. A squirrel ran over the white icing, into our yard, and up the black bark trunk of our cherry tree.

The huge Danish pastry looked sweet. I grabbed the center metal strip and a window latch from the left side window and leaned far out. My hand slid from the center strip, and my torso and knees slipped out the window. I held the latch tightly with my left hand and grabbed the top of the window with my other hand as it turned on its hinges toward the outside. My ankles caught the center metal strip and my legs pulled hard against it; the window and I moved slowly back inside. When my knees were safe, I grabbed the center metal strip and pushed myself safely onto the window seat. I sat there seat for several minutes, breathed hard and tried to gain some composure.

Did I slip out, or did I let myself slip out?

The answer eluded me, and the question frightened me.

* * *

Wednesday, 12:45 p.m.

Over a hundred people have gathered at Jenny's Restaurant and Bar. Loud chatter mixes with the incongruent smell of cigarette smoke and home-cooking.

I sip on my tall-glass Manhattan and mentally prepare my thank-you-for-coming after-dinner speech. Although I enjoy public speaking, a tinge of nervousness always gnaws at me about an hour before I speak. Thoughts about my mother's confidence in me have often quelled my uneasiness. Where, I wonder, will that confidence and calming come from now?

A large, heavy, shaking hand squeezes my shoulder. Ray supports himself with one hand on his walker and the other on me. He smiles and says, "Hey, Big Jim."

* * *

I closed and latched the outside windows, and replaced the storm window. I crawled into my bed and pulled the blankets tightly over me. I shivered and shook...but not from the cold.

After about a half hour, the folding door at the bottom of the stairwell slapped open. The light fixture over the hallway and stairs illuminated and my mother's voice resonated up the stairwell. "Go on up. He's feeling much better."

I thought she might be talking to Mike, but the footsteps weren't the light skipping steps of a kid, but a heavy deliberate clomping up the stairs. I peered out from my bed, through my doorway, down the hall and at the top of the stairwell.

Ray's blond slicked-back hair emerged from the top of the stairs. His huge body, silhouetted by the light fixture, stood at the end of the hallway. In spite of winter, he wore a short-sleeved sport shirt, the sleeves rolled up tightly just above his bulging biceps and rose tattoo. He walked down the hallway toward my room and stopped by the dark doorway of Beth's room.

"Big Jim?" he whispered into the empty room.

"Down here, Ray." I directed him to the far end of the hall.

He walked into my darkened room and cackled, "What's this bullshit of bein' sick on your birthday?"

"I don't know," I answered and forced a phony laugh.
He plopped down on the window seat.

"Man, I remember my seventeenth birthday. Some
guy said somethin' to my girlfriend, so I tried to throw him
out of a second-story window at Thornton High School. I got
suspended for two weeks! Great birthday present. Then my
girl turned around—"

"Ray, you afraid of dyin'?"

"Huh?"

"You ever think about dyin'?"

"What're ya' talkin' about?"

It was as if another person inside me had rehearsed
a speech, taken over my body, and begun speaking. I told him
everything. I told him about Mr. Charleston, my grandfather's wake, Mary, the effects of the fire and plane crash on
me—everything.

He stared through me for several seconds, then asked,
"You tell your mom and dad about all this?"

"No," I whispered. "I...can't."

Ray looked down and nodded. That was enough
explanation for him; he had the same mistrust for authority as
I.

He turned from me and watched out the window for a
few minutes. He seemed to have moved far away and into his
own thoughts.

"Yeah," he finally spoke at the window, "I used to
think about death a lot—right after my mother died." He
faced in my general direction. "I wasn't much older
than you. I didn't think about death right away; I just thought
about her. I would cry myself to sleep every night. My old
man just ignored me. Then I started thinking about dyin' and

what it would be like if I died. Ya' know, wonderin' if I'd see her again. That's when the nightmares started. It got bad. I never told anyone this, but a couple times I thought about doin' myself in, endin' it all."

"Yeah?"

"Yeah."

"Well, how…I mean what happened or what did you do about it?"

That's when he giggled to himself and looked down again.

"Funny, man. That's what's funny. School and me never got along, but it was somethin' in school that brought me through it. In sixth grade the nun gave us this book to read by a guy named Mark Twain. Even before the first chapter there was a page with just one saying on it. I'll always remember it. It said: *The fear of death follows from the fear of life. A man who lives fully is prepared to die at any time.*"

We sat in silence as I let the words sink into my brain.

"What's it mean?" I asked.

Another silence.

"Shit, I don't know! I never got past the third page of the book."

I laughed out loud. This was a true laugh, not phony, and it felt good.

"What I *do* know is from that moment on I started livin' and stopped worrin' about dyin'. I tried to enjoy every-thing about life; I still do, probably too much for a guy with a wife and a kid on the way."

I swung my legs over the side of my bed, placed my bare feet on the warm tile floor, took a couple of short strides toward my built-in desk, and pulled the short copper chain of the desk lamp. As the long fluorescent lamp warmed from dim to brightness, Ray shaded his eyes and asked, "What the hell are you doin'?"

I opened the spiral notebook to a blank page, picked up a sharp pencil and asked, "What was that saying again?"

He repeated it several times slowly, and I copied it on the blank page, closed the notebook, turned off the light, and hopped back into bed.

"Thanks, Ray."

"For what? Anyway, I better get out of here before you sneeze leprosy, the clap, or whatever you got, and I catch it. Besides, I got an open bottle of Schlitz gettin' warm downstairs. Take care, Big Jim!"

He squeezed my shoulder, stood up, and walked through the doorway into the lighted hall. His heavy footsteps lumbered down the stairs, and the folding door slapped shut.

Chapter 30

The sign inside the window read:
Princeton Music School
Opening Soon
Sign up Now
For 3 Free Lessons!
Wow, I thought, a message from God!

The thin layer of snow that had covered the main street of Riverdale the night before was scraped into narrow dirty white piles along the curb and the median by the huge blade of the snowplow. Our '53 Nash idled between the dirty piles of snow at the lone stop sign on 144th Street. I pointed across my mother's face to the sign in the storefront window of the half-block-long single-story building, "Look, Mom! The sign, three free lessons!"

She focused on it as if more information would magically appear, until the driver in the car behind us beeped his horn.

"We'll talk to your dad about it."

That was enough to squelch my enthusiasm. Big Lou had a knack for finding the negative side of everything.

It had been several weeks since my birthday. Every day since my talk with Ray, I awoke with a more positive attitude and a *carpe diem* outlook. The rhythm of rock and roll music stirred me again, and I played my 45s over and over. Playing those records rekindled my enthusiasm for playing the drums.

After dinner I looked at Mom to see if this was a good time to bring up the drum lessons. She gave me "the nod."

"Dad, there's a new music school opening up on 144th Street. They're offerin' three free lessons. Can I start takin' drum lessons again?"

He looked at me with a strange smile as if he knew something that I didn't and said, "Nothin's free, son."

"No, Dad, the sign said, 'three free lessons.' No kiddin'!"

"Nothin's free, kid."

He reached for his pack of Salems, walked to the living room, and settled into his lounge chair for the evening.

I sat and glared at my plate. My mother picked up the dishes and whispered to me, "Don't worry. I'll work on him tonight."

Sunday morning I tried to oversleep, so I could avoid going to Sunday school. As usual, my mother saw through the scheme and routinely sent Terri upstairs with a wet rag to slap across my face.

I sat down at my place at the kitchen table to greet, in my opinion, the worst day of the week. Mom was making French toast while Terri, Beth, and I sat in Sunday morning silence. My father read the sports section of the Sunday paper and drank his coffee.

.   While flipping slices of Wonder Bread in a bowl of beaten eggs my mother said to Big Lou, "Well, why don't you tell him?"

"Huh?" he answered, still reading the sports section.
"You know."

I don't know what Mom had said or had done, but he put the paper down and said, "Oh yeah, we decided to let you try that three free lessons thing."

I perked up immediately. My first instinct was to run over and hug him, but then I remembered that he frowned on that stuff with me.

"Yay, Dad! Thanks!"

"Just remember what I said," he lectured while trying not to show any emotion. "Nothin's free."

Monday, Mom picked me up after school, and we drove to Princeton Music School. Although the place didn't officially open until the following week, the door was open and the inside was all lit up. As soon as we walked in a little energetic man in a tailored dark suit almost magically appeared.

"Welcome, welcome, Lieberstein's the name! How can I help you fine people?"

"Well, my son would like to take drum lessons and—"

"Excellent! Excellent! Sit down. Sit down."

We sat on a long wooden bench just inside the doorway. Across from us Mr. Lieberstein sat on a stool behind a glass case counter. The glass case displayed small musical items such as harmonicas, mouthpieces for various horns, guitar picks, and drumsticks. Hanging displays of guitars, banjos, and horns lined the rest of the room, and floor displays of organs and drum sets glimmered beneath the fluorescent lights. It looked more like a music store than a music school.

Whenever Mom could squeeze in a few sentences, she explained that I had taken lessons a few years earlier with J.P. Mr. Lieberstein, however, did most of the talking. He explained the "no obligation" three free lessons and raved about the great instructors at the school.

He set me up with Thursday night lessons at 7 o'clock starting the following week. My instructor would be a guy named Mr. Crossley. Before we left, he reached inside the glass display case, pulled out a miniature harmonica, and gave it to me.

"As a token of my gratitude for choosing Princeton Music School, Louis," he said like an uncle giving his favorite nephew some spending money.

"Thank you, sir."

It was a rather generous gift. It wasn't exactly a real harmonica, but it wasn't a toy either. As soon as I accepted it I heard Big Lou's voice in my head, "Nothin's free, kid."

All week I worked on my beginner drumming skills; I worked on sitting straight, holding the sticks, striking the practice pad, and reading the notes. Before long I was "1-e-and-a-2-e-and-a"ing just like two years earlier.

Mom dropped me off in front of Princeton Music School at about 6:55 p.m. that Thursday. The plan was that she would shop at the small department store down the street for about a half hour and then pick me up.

I walked inside with my drumsticks in hand. Mr. Lieberstein approached me as if I were his long-lost son.

"Louis! Louis!" he said, extending his hand in a warm handshake. "Great to see you, son. Mr. Crossley's waiting in the studio room."

We walked through a hallway with several doors on each side, all closed, but I could hear faint talking and single notes played on either a piano or a trumpet behind the doors. At the end of the hallway a doorway led to a spacious studio room, the size of a small basketball court. A beige upright piano, several electric guitars resting against amplifiers, and various black horn cases resembling the shapes of the trumpets, trombones, and saxophones presumably inside occupied the center space.

The most prominent instrument, however, was the beautiful white pearl Slingerland drum set near the wall on the left. A wooden bench extended along the wall, the full length of the room. A guy in his mid-to-late forties sat on the bench near the drum set. He had sandy grayish hair and dressed in a blue long-sleeved sport shirt, khaki pants, and Hush Puppies. He sat with one foot on the bench and tucked closely to his body, while the other foot dangled lazily beneath. All the while he puffed on a cigarette. A half-filled cup of coffee rested on the bench beside him. The coffee and cigarette reminded me of J.P

"Hey, Croz!" Mr. Lieberstein called out.

The guy turned his head lazily and squinted through the blue smoke he had blown through his nose. Even after the smoke cleared he still squinted, probably from some kind of smoky haze still in his head.

As we approached him, he stood up as if his body rejected his attempt to stand and put the cigarette between his lips to free his hand for a handshake.

"Louis, this is Mr. Crossley; Croz, this is Louis, the kid I was telling you about."

"Pleased to meet ya', kid," he said and extended his hand.

"Well," Mr. Lieberstein said as he turned and walked away, "I'll leave you two 'Gene Krupas' alone."

"Sit down, kid," Mr. Crossley said, indicating the stool behind the drum set.

I did so and positioned the snare drum perfectly, but I didn't think he noticed.

"So ya' had some lessons before, huh?"

"Yes, sir, Mr.Crossley."

"Let's forget that 'Mr.Crossley' crap. Just call me 'Croz.' Well, let's see what ya' know."

He took a music stand from the center of the room, placed it in front of the drum set, and positioned it so I could view the tray of the stand. Then he placed a book entitled *The Beginner Drummer* on the tray and opened it to pages four and five.

"Start playing from page four and keep going until ya' get to a page that seems too hard."

The first few pages were easy—just quarter notes: right, left, left, right, right, right, left, left, etc. Then, the exercises progressed to eighth notes, sixteenth notes, until the combinations and symbols were too difficult for me.

He sensed my struggle and closed the book.

"Okay, okay, kid, we'll start each session with warm-ups from this book. I'll teach ya' a new page or so for you to practice at home and we'll move on from there. We'll do that shit for about twenty minutes or so, and then we'll jam a little."

"Jam a little?" I asked.

"Yeah. Ya' ever use brushes before?"

"No, Mr. Cross—...Croz."

"Put those sticks down on the bench."

He picked up two metal stick-like contraptions resting on a metal rib of the base drum. Pushing the ends of each metal contraption produced a fan-like brush of stiff thin metal brushes. He handed them to me and said, "Take this one in your left hand and make small circles with the brushes on the snare."

I followed his instructions and produced a swishing sound.

"Now," he continued, "hit the snare with the other brush on each count of 1-and-2-and-3-and-4-and."

It was kind of like rubbing my stomach and patting my head at the same time, so I caught on quickly.

"Okay, on the '1, 2, 3, 4' hit the bass with your right foot."

That was easy. J.P. had taught me to always keep time with my right foot.

"Yeah, okay," Croz complimented, "now on '2' and '4' close the high-hat cymbals with your left foot.

This final combination was much more difficult, and it took me several minutes of practice to put it all together.

When I finally got the whole thing down fairly well, Croz crept over to the piano and started playing *Tea for Two*. I adjusted my playing to his rhythm, and we played *Tea for Two* several times.

Then Croz stopped abruptly and looked at his watch. "Okay, kid, time's up. Ya' did alright, yeah, alright."

When I got up to leave, he startled me when he said, "Oh, wait! I almost forgot this fuckin' thing." He stood up, reached into his shirt pocket, and pulled out a three-by-five card. After making a mark on it, he handed it to me and said, "On your way out give this to *Lichtenstein* or whatever the hell his name is."

On my way to the door, I looked at the card. The words *Princeton School Report Card* appeared at the top. Halfway down the card were spaces for the date and a grade.

Croz had given me an 'A+.'

When I handed the card to Mr. Lieberstein, he barely looked at it and said, "Fantastic! Fantastic! How was your first lesson?"

"Great! I learned how to use the brushes."

"Super! Do you have a pair to practice with?"

"No, sir."

He reached inside the glass counter display, pulled out a pair of metal brushes just like those I had used during the lesson, and gave them to me.

"A gift from me to you."

"Thank you, sir," I said, but my father's words echoed in my head again, "Nothin's free, kid."

All week I practiced diligently. The practice pad wouldn't work with the brushes. The rubber center wasn't smooth, so the left brush wouldn't make small circles. I used the smooth cover from an old scratched Ricky Nelson album, and it worked perfectly.

The following Thursday I was eager to get started. When I walked into the studio, Croz looked exactly like he did a week earlier—same position, same clothes. I almost thought that Mr. Lieberstein kept him captive in there, giving him coffee, cigarettes, and occasionally a bowl of food.

He turned as I walked toward him.

"Hey, kid, welcome back."

I warmed up by playing some of the pages he had given me for homework. After about fifteen minutes of that, he went over to the piano and played *Tea for Two* again. I kept time with the brushes, snare drum, bass drum, and high-hat routine that I had practiced all week.

"Alright, kid, somethin' new," he announced as he left the piano. "Put the brushes down and grab the sticks. You're gonna' learn the rock and roll beat. With the right stick, tap the cymbal to '1-and-2-and-3-and-4-and.' At the same time, keep time on the bass drum on '1' and '3' only."

No problem.

"Now, on '2-and' and '4,' strike the snare with your left stick."

That was more difficult, but I caught on quickly.

"Okay, with your left foot, close the high-hat on '2' and '4.'"

That was almost too much, but after several trial-and-errors I got it down.

When Croz thought I knew it well enough, he picked up one of the electric guitars and turned on its amplifier. After tuning it up, he said, "When I nod, you come in with what you just learned."

He played the introduction to *Rock Around the Clock*, then nodded, and I joined in. We played the song all the way through, but a little slower than normal so I could keep up with him.

"Okay, kid, that's it."

I handed in my 'A+' and went home.

Practicing without a cymbal challenged my imagination. I took an old drumstick and lodged it in my top dresser drawer so that it stood straight up. The bead of the stick fit perfectly through the center hole of the scratched Ricky Nelson album, and *voila*—a cymbal! As long as I didn't tap the album too hard and break it, my practice sessions continued.

Knowing that my last free lesson was coming up, I tried to show Big Lou that I was practicing really hard, so he would consider paying for more. The strategy seemed to pay off. He was softening up a little, even though he was well aware that the *3 Free Lessons* was a come-on. The cost of more lessons wasn't exorbitant, and he even admitted that his "Nothin's free" philosophy may have been overstated.

My third session went along routinely; I started with warm-ups, and then moved on to the brushes. This time he taught me how to use the cymbal and tom-toms with the brushes during the rests and interludes of *Tea for Two*. Similarly, he taught me to play the drum introduction part to *Rock Around the Clock* and short drum rolls around the tom-toms and snare during the drum breaks called "fill-ins."

When I had finished the session I felt as if I could play with any band, as long as the band only played *Tea for Two* and *Rock Around the Clock*.

As I handed in my third 'A+,' Mr. Lieberstein asked, "So, we'll be seeing you next Thursday night, right?"

"I'm pretty sure, sir."

"Well, I'll *make* sure," he said. "Is your family at home most week nights?"

I nodded.

"Good, have a good night!"

I didn't know what he had meant, but I didn't think any more about it.

The following Tuesday, after supper, the phone rang. Mom answered, "Hello...Oh...Well, that's wonderful... Yes...That's okay...We'll see you then...Good-bye."

"That was Mr. Lieberstein," she informed us with a slightly cynical tone to her voice. "You were chosen as *The Student of the Month*."

"Congratulations," Big Lou said to me with a very skeptical look on his face.

"He's coming over to talk to us at about seven," Mom added.

Expressionless, he returned to his comfort zone, the lounge chair in front of the TV.

At seven o'clock sharp, Mr. Lieberstein rang the front doorbell. Big Lou answered the door.

"Congratulations! Congratulations! Congratulations!" Mr. Lieberstein said to him as he opened the screen door himself, walked right in, and shook my father's hand. "Oh, I almost forgot. Can you give me a hand with this?" He walked outside again, and Big Lou followed and carried a large but seemingly lightweight black box by its handle, and Mr. Lieberstein carried a black leather briefcase. "Just set that in the middle of the room," he ordered as if he had rented out our house, and my father were the bellboy.

Big Lou was clearly annoyed.

"Well," said Mr. Lieberstein as he sat himself on our couch, and we followed, "I just wanted to show you how far Louis has progressed in just three lessons!"

He opened the big black box. A snare drum with its folded stand, a cymbal with its folded stand, a pair of drumsticks, and a 45-rpm record neatly filled the box. He quickly set up the snare and cymbal. Then he pulled up a nearby chair and sat me behind the drum. He picked up the record, pointed at the Hi-Fi, and asked, "May I?"

My mother nodded.

"Okay, Louis. Just like Mr. Crossley taught you."

He started the record *Rock Around the Clock* by Bill Haley and the Comets:

> *One, two three o'clock, four o'clock, rock,*
> *Five, six, seven o'clock, eight o'clock, rock,*
> *Nine, ten, eleven o'clock, twelve o'clock, rock,*
> *We're gonna' rock around the clock tonight.*

I played the introduction along with the record and kept the beat going on the cymbal and snare including drum rolls during the fill-ins. When the record finished, I thought I had done a pretty impressive job. My parents looked more cynical than proud.

"As both of you can tell, Louis has progressed unbelievably in just three lessons. I was thinking of putting together a little combo of my prodigies, which of course would include Louis. I can book them for little gigs around the area."

Big Lou's facial expression transformed from cynicism to a definite frown.

"The problem is that Louis needs some sophisticated equipment to match his talent." He reached into his black leather briefcase and pulled out two catalogues: one labeled *Ludwig* and the other labeled *Slingerland*. He opened each catalogue to a specific page and handed them to my parents. "Come over here, Louis, and show your good parents which drum sets you like."

I went behind the couch and looked between them at the pictures. The sets were beautiful. Flat, shiny, sparkle, and pearl colors highlighted each set on the page. My focus was on the beauty of these instruments; Mom and Big Lou focused on the prices, which started at $500 and went up with each turn of a page.

In his most dignified tone, my father expressed his concerns. "I wasn't expecting prices like these. Can he still take the lessons without the drum sets?"

"Well…uh…I suppose so…but…uh…with the skills he'll be learning from now on, he would need a set of drums. Now, we could rent out our equipment, but…uh…at that cost it would be less expensive to simply purchase one of these fine sets…"

"But you see at these prices, I'm not prepared to—"

"Please, please," Mr. Lieberstein said as if he understood perfectly, "if it's a question of money, we can arrange something."

"My wife and I will have to discuss this in private," he answered.

"Go right ahead. Take your time. Louis, his beautiful sisters, and I will just visit a while."

"No, you don't understand," he tried again. "We need some time to discuss this and—"

"Look, pick out any set from either book, and I'll knock 10% right off the top!"

Big Lou's voice grew tense. "I think you'd better leave now. We'll contact you with our decision."

Mr. Lieberstein finally sensed my father's agitation and backed off. "Of course, sure, talk it over! Talk it over!" He packed up the drum equipment and briefcase as Big Lou showed him to the door. Before he left, he turned and said, "I'll call tomorrow night and see if you've made a decision. Have a nice evening. By the way, you have a lovely little house."

After he closed the door, Big Lou turned to me and said in an I-told-you-so tone, "Nothing's free. Let's sit down and talk."

We (Mom, Beth, Terri, and I) squeezed onto the couch. Dad pulled up a chair and sat in front of us.

"I can't afford this," he put it simply.

"But Dad, I—"

"There's no 'but Dad' about it. Do you have any idea how many hours I have to work in the steel mill to earn $500 or more?"

I had no idea; I was a kid.

"Can't we—"

"No. Sorry. Besides, I don't want my kid playing in some gin mill somewhere."

I did what any kid my age would have done...I pouted. I looked toward Mom for her sympathy and possibly her I'll-work-on-him-later look, but she just frowned and nodded her agreement with him.

With that, I stomped upstairs and went to bed, but I didn't sleep...I pouted.

The next day I went to school and pouted there.

Then I came home, went up to my room, and pouted some more. At dinner, I pouted and gave Big Lou the silent treatment, the 'hurt little kid' act, as if that bothered him.

After dinner I went upstairs to my room again and routinely pretended to do homework. At about 7:30 the phone rang. The kitchen phone was the only one in the house, so my mother nearly always answered it.

"Hello...Yes...No, we decided not to...No, it's not that. We just don't think he's ready for this...Uh huh..."

By this time I was downstairs in the kitchen watching her talk to him.

"Yes, he's here…Well, I don't know if…" She looked down at me. "Fine," she said into the receiver and handed the phone to me. "He wants to talk to you."

"Hello?" I said.

"Louis, this is Mr. Lieberstein. Your mom tells me you won't be continuing your lessons here."

I didn't say anything.

"Listen," he said in a hushed voiced, "if your family is having financial problems, we can work something out. We have financing that…"

I stopped listening. His words hit me where no one had ever hit me before…in my pride. He was calling us poor. I walked a few steps and looked out the dining room window and across the alley. The lights in Mike's TV room were on. It reminded me of my first drum lesson with J.P. He taught me to play drums because he wanted me to be a good drummer—because he thought drumming was important and a drummer should do it right.

Lieberstein had probably coached Crossley to teach me some easy flashy stuff, so he could impress my parents and sell them an expensive drum set they couldn't afford.

"Louis? Louis, are you still there?"

"Uh…ye-yes, sir, Mr. Lieberstein. Mr. Lieberstein, my mom and dad are right. I'm not ready for this. Excuse me. I have to do my homework."

I handed the receiver back to my mother and walked into the living room. My father had dozed off in his lounge chair; the TV provided the only light as it reflected and flashed off his tired body. Hours of working in the steel mill had drained him. He rested peacefully.

Perhaps I could take lessons somewhere else, I thought. Perhaps I could hook up with Croz at another music school...all that could wait for now. There was something that I knew I had to do.

"Dad...Dad?"

"Huh? Whu'..." He shook his head, but remained in a daze.

"You were right, Dad...You were right," I whispered.

" 'Bout what?" he asked as he rubbed his eyes with one hand and reached for his glasses with the other.

"You were right...Nothin's free...Nothin's free."

He put his glasses on and stared at me like he was seeing someone for the first time.

I knew that what I was going to do next would embarrass both of us, but I did it anyway. I walked up to him and hugged him around his neck...After a few long seconds, I felt Big Lou's warm calloused hand gently pat me on my back.

Chapter 31

I stood up, and Big Lou stared uncomfortably at the TV screen. As I started to leave the living room, he motioned for me to sit on the couch, and he got up and turned the sound down on the set. The Beave on *Leave It To Beaver* scrunched up his face and mouthed an explanation for some predicament to June and Ward Cleaver.

"Look," my father said as he plopped back into his lounge chair, "This doesn't mean the end of this drum business. Maybe you can earn some money over the summer and fall, and maybe by the winter we can afford equipment and the lessons and do this drum thing right."

"Okay, Dad."

This was the first time Big Lou spoke to me with a measure of respect—the way Ray spoke to me.

As the winter snow and ice melted away, my pouting and yearning to play the drums melted away, also.

In 1959 most public school kids in the Chicago suburbs were on break from March 27th (Good Friday) through Sunday, April 5th. By Monday, March 30th, Mike, Rick, and I had run out of things to do. We decided to walk to the train trestle, cross the Little Calumet River, and go roller skating at

Art's Roller Rink in Harvey. When we got there our plans collapsed. Illinois Central Railroad construction workers were replacing railroad ties and rails atop the trestle. Crossing the river was impossible.

The Little Calumet River and its alleged raw sewage bordered the southwest corner of Riverdale from Halsted Street on the west to the train trestle on the east. From the trestle, the river curved southward bordering a thin strip of Dolton on its east side and the "backyard" of Harvey on its west side.

We sat down on a dry pile of stones dumped at the base of the trestle. The workers would be spreading the stones around the newly laid railroad track. The temperature was about 38 degrees, and dirty patches of snow still littered the brown grass wherever shadows lingered for most of the day. On the riverbank, thin ice spread toward the middle of the river until it finally surrendered to the green current of the murky water.

Kids from the Midwest were well educated about the dangers of playing around early spring ice. The schools showed safety films about how to build a human chain to rescue someone who had fallen through thin ice into a cold river, lake, or deep pond. Even daredevil Rick respected the danger of playing on ice during this time of year.

We sat on the pile of stones for about a half hour playing a game whereby we would see who could toss a stone and get it as close to the edge of the ice without it tumbling into the near freezing green water. As if inspired by a brilliant idea, Rick jumped up and just blurted out, "Let's walk down the river to the witch's house!"

"What!" I said in disbelief.

"Are you crazy?" Mike added. "We're not even supposed to be by the river. My dad told me not to wander off
this far…especially around *that* house."

The area east of the river in Dolton was a thickly
wooded area known unofficially as Witch's Woods. The
name "Witch's Woods" never appeared on a Dolton, a
Chicago area, or an Illinois state map. The name evolved
from its only resident who lived in an old rotting frame house
buried deep in the woods. Very few people ever saw the
woman who lived there, so naturally, just as the "Boo Radley"
legend in Harper Lee's *To Kill a Mockingbird* grew, the legend that the woman living there was a witch grew also.

Stories about the woman nurtured the legend throughout the years. Tales spread of unidentified human remains
found in the vicinity. The most notorious tale was that of two
missing kids who were last seen snooping around her house
and then mysteriously disappeared one summer in the mid
1940s. The police allegedly searched the area including the
witch's house, but they didn't find a trace of evidence.
Rumor had it that the old woman cackled and mocked the
police as they tore apart her house and searched for leads.

"C'mon chickenshits," Rick urged. "Who's gonna'
know? Besides, we'll say we got lost. We were walkin' along
the riverbank, just tryin' to find our way, and we ran into her
house. I've never seen her house. Have you guys?"

"No," I said, "but I've heard about it. I heard there are
animals' and even people's skeletons buried between the river
and her house."

"I don't know," Mike shook his head. "Remember
that tape recording Paul and his friend Bob made?"

Paul was an older kid who lived next door to me. The previous summer he and his buddy, Bob, had sat on Paul's front porch and listened to a reel-to-reel tape recorder.

Paul called to us, "Hey, you guys wanna' hear somethin'?"

We walked up the two steps from the lane to his front porch. Paul and Bob were just smiling, nodding, and listening. Tinny treble sounds of someone walking inside a room, perhaps a kitchen, and putting dishes away vibrated from the speaker. During this activity a woman spoke incoherently. Then, after some silence, echoes of high-pitched screaming erupted from the speaker.

"What the hell are we listening to?" I asked.

"The witch," Bob said.

"What?"

"Bob stayed overnight last night," Paul had said, "and we snuck out with this battery powered tape recorder. We went into Witch's Woods and put a microphone in her broken basement window. Then we turned the machine to 'record' and let it run for about a half hour."

"Wow!" we said.

"So what's that screamin' about?" Mike asked.

"She just sits in her basement and screams," Paul replied.

So that was the tape.

"That tape was bullcrap," Rick said while we sat on the pile of stones.

"Maybe, and maybe not," I said, "but we don't have anything better to do…Let's go."

Mike agreed, and we began our journey starting beneath the trestle on the riverbank. At that point the river flowed eastward, but gradually bent southward toward Sibley Boulevard. The witch's house was about a half mile from the trestle and a block before the Sibley Boulevard overpass.

After about twenty minutes of tedious hiking we saw a small clearing at the riverbank ahead. We approached it like hunters stalking wild game. A narrow path emerged in the middle of the wooded edge of the clearing. The path curved just enough into the thick woods so that its endpoint was invisible...but we knew where it led.

We didn't speak a word. Rick moved first and headed toward the path; Mike and I followed. Some flagstones must have been thrown hastily along the path many years before because they were barely visible from years of muddy water washing over them.

After about twenty yards the path ended abruptly at a larger clearing. To the right some old rotting porch steps came into view. The steps led to the back porch of a small dilapidated farmhouse. The wood on the house had rotted into a grayish-brown color. Small-paned windows peered from the wall on each side of the back porch door. Yellowed newspaper covered the inside window glass. The back porch door was the kind of door that people used indoors to close off rooms. It had rotted and splintered from exposure to the outside elements. A simple brass knob protruded from the right side of the door about halfway up. A huge round stone and cement fireplace covered about two-thirds of the west wall. The fireplace tapered upward into a beautiful chimney with red and gray round stones neatly mortared together. The rest of the house seemed to be desperately clinging to this beautiful strong structure.

This was where the witch lived, and the witch was home. Burning damp cottonwood spit small red sparks and puffs of gray smoke out the chimney. No broken basement windows lined the base of the house as Paul and Bob had informed us; there was no basement at all.

We just stood in the clearing and stared at the house. A woman's voice called out, but not the shrieking old lady voice that talked and screamed on the audio tape; it was just a woman's voice calling from inside the house, "What do you boys want?"

All three of us gasped at the same time, and our eyes focused on the simple brass knob on the back porch door that turned like the second hand of a large clock. We didn't want to see what was on the other side, so we let our imaginations see it: an old hag with stringy hair, no teeth, warts and pockmarks on her face. She was hunched over in a gunnysack-like dress, and she was pointing a shotgun at us. Then our imaginations said, "Run like hell!"

In my younger days I had the gift of speed, and I used it at that moment to a fault. I raced ahead of Mike and Rick down the flagstone path. When I reached the small clearing a shocking reality hit me; the river came next. I tried desperately to stop at the bank, but my momentum kept me moving. I instinctively did a baseball "hook" slide onto the thin ice. I felt the cold water seep from its surface through my pants.

By this time Mike and Rick had reached the small clearing and stared in disbelief at what they saw. I must have looked like the drowning kid in the safety film from school. I hoped that they would remember the part in the film where the people formed a human chain to save the kid, but all they did was stand on the riverbank and scream, "Ahhhhh!"

When I realized that screaming "Ahhhhh!" wasn't helping, I formulated a plan. The sheet of ice had stabilized, but it cracked a little more every time I inched forward toward the riverbank about four yards away. I knew that somehow I had to get to my feet and leap forward. I pulled my knees to my chest and positioned the toes of my shoes onto the ice. As I stood up I could see the ice crack like a lightning bolt beneath my left foot and toward the riverbank. With all the strength in my legs I sprang forward.

My right foot found enough traction, but my left went straight through the ice. My body shot forward at an angle. Mike and Rick were at the edge of the riverbank, and they grabbed the wrist and forearm of my right arm and pulled me into the small clearing.

The three of us rested in that little clearing for several minutes. Only our heavy breaths broke the cold silence. Too much adrenalin had pumped through our systems in too short a time. I sat up and looked at my feet.

"Oh shit," I said. The shock and excitement had masked the fact that my left shoe was gone, and my foot was freezing. The shoe must have come off when I leaped forward and my foot went through the ice. Surely the current had carried it away. "Now what am I gonna' do?"

We worked on some stories that I could tell my parents, but even we couldn't make ourselves believe them. Then Mike stood up and said, "Maybe we can think of somethin' on the way home. Why don't you take your undershirt off and wrap it around your foot. At least you'll be able to walk home on it."

That seemed like a good idea. When I stood up to take my coat off something curious appeared. An old black rubber boot, not necessarily a man's or a woman's, just an old black rubber boot stood on a muddy sunken flagstone at the beginning of the path. I walked toward the boot, and Mike and Rick followed. A grayish-looking rag protruded from the top opening of the boot. I bent down and picked it up. It was an old but very clean gray woolen sock.

I turned to Mike and Rick. "Do ya' think....?"

"Who else could've left it?" Mike said.

"Should I thank her?" I asked.

"Hell no!" Rick said. "I'm not even sure you should put 'em on. There might be a bat in there ready to bite your toe off!"

I didn't care. My foot was freezing, and I was willing to take the risk. I took my cold, wet, dirty sock off my foot and threw it in the river. When I pulled the wool sock over my cold foot I immediately felt the warmth returning to it. Then I slipped my covered foot into the boot, which was a little too big, as if it had belonged to an older kid or a small adult woman.

Mike and Rick were already making the return trip down the riverbank. "Come on, let's go," Mike turned and coached me. "We're already in trouble for bein' gone so long!"

I looked up the flagstone trail. I yelled, "Thank you!"

I waited a few seconds, but no answer came, so I joined Mike and Rick for the long trip home.

After about an hour we arrived in front of my house where Mike and Rick departed for home. In all that time we hadn't come up with a believable story for my lost shoe and sock.

As I stood in the middle of the sidewalk and stared at my front door a unique idea hit me. I decided to attempt a new strategy for situations like this; I would tell the truth. Sure! It always worked on *Leave It to Beaver*. Whenever the Beave got into trouble the same scenario repeated itself. Beaver sat on the living room couch or his twin bed while his parents, Ward and June Cleaver, sat by him. He would tell his parents what had happened as Ward and June listened with raised eyebrows. When Beaver finished, Ward would say something such as, "Well, Beaver, I hope you learned your lesson, and I do commend you for telling the truth."

Beaver would scrunch up his face and say something funny in his innocent-1950s-kid voice (canned laughter). Then June would say to him, "Now go upstairs and wash up before dinner, dear." When Beaver left, June would say, "W-a-a-a-a-a-rd, do you think Beaver really learned his lesson?"

Ward would briefly reminisce about a similar experience from his own childhood with a humorous tagline. More canned laughter, music up, and then the show would cut to a commercial.

Everything would be perfect. My parents would just have to know their lines.

I immediately sensed that I was not in the Cleaver household when I walked through the front door.

"Where in the hell have you been!" Big Lou yelled.

"And what happened to your shoe?" Mom added.

I didn't panic. I sat down on the living room couch and waited for them to sit, too. Then I told them the whole story. I even scrunched my face up a few times, just like the Beave. When I looked up, it seemed to have worked. My father had that concerned Ward Cleaver look on his face, and Mom wore her I'm-trying-to-understand face.

But after a few beats of silence they reminded me again that this was not the Cleaver household.

"How many times have we told you to stay away from that river?"

"Where do you get off thinking you can go snoopin' around a person's house like that? Now get your sorry butt upstairs *without dinner* while your mother and I come up with a good punishment for this bullshit you came home with!"

So much for the truth and the *Leave It to Beaver* approach.

Spring finally arrived about three weeks later. Lawns grew green and ready for mowing. Mom's flower garden started to bloom, and she worried that an early spring frost might ruin it.

We were having dinner one night around this time when Big Lou threw out his usual school night question, "Well, how was school today?"

This time Beth, my older sister, didn't offer her stock "It was okay" answer. Instead, she said "We went to the witch's house today."

"What?" Mom asked.

Beth mockingly replied very slowly, "W-e-e w-e-e-n-t t-o the w-i-i-tch-e-e-s—"

"Don't get smart, young lady!" Big Lou interrupted.

"Miss Dumont, our science teacher," Beth continued, "said that the woman who lived by the river was some kind of expert on wildflowers and all that nature stuff. Miss Dumont knows her. Anyway, it's only a few blocks from school, so she walked our whole class over there. Everyone was scared, but she made us go. We didn't stay long, but the woman showed us all these flowers and plants around her house and talked about the animals that lived by the river. She was pretty nice to us. Her name is Miss Verhoeven or something like that."

Big Lou seemed more interested in his dinner than her story by now but asked, "Well, what did you learn?"

Beth's answer, though anti-climactic, never went further than our dinner table. No one in Riverdale wanted to hear it or to believe it anyway.

"That lady....who lives in Witch's Woods....she's no witch."

Chapter 32

My parents grounded me for two weeks as a consequence of the Witch's Woods incident—a just punishment. It ended on April 13th, and on the following Saturday Riverdale and Dolton held Little League tryouts. Trying out for Little League was a rite of passage for an eight-year-old Riverdale male just like a first communion for a Catholic or a Bar Mitzvah for a Jew.

My tryout went badly. I missed several fly balls and didn't hit the ball very well. If a kid didn't get a call from a team manager by the next Saturday at noon, he knew that he wasn't on a Little League team.

By 1:00 p.m., Saturday, I hadn't been called. Jentz, Loll, Pews, and Smitty had gotten calls during the week from Little League managers.

Beth was out somewhere with one of her friends. My parents and Terri were shopping at Sears, Big Lou's favorite hangout. He could spend hours in the Sears hardware department just picking up tools and playing with them.

I was alone.

* * *

Wednesday, 1:15 p.m.

"Excuse me! Excuse me!" A distraught young wait-ress beckons me toward the bar. She tosses her long blond hair behind her shoulders and exposes small delicate facial features that wrinkle with tension as she speaks. "Mr. Macaluso, we have a *big* problem."

"What is it?" I ask; the effects of my Manhattan have started to kick in.

"You told us that around seventy people would be eat-ing. There are over a hundred!"

"Do you have enough food?"

"Yes."

"Do you have enough room?"

"Well, we can set some more tables, but it's gonna' cost more."

"I expected that; so what's the problem?"

She sighs, turns, and walks through the swinging metal door and into the kitchen.

This confrontation alerts me that it's time to direct people to their tables. As I politely ask groups to be seated, I am modestly amazed at the variety of people—relatives, Mom's friends from her church, childhood friends, high school friends, acquaintances, and some former neighbors from the old neighborhood on Glen Lane. Specifically, Mr. Stewart showed up with Mrs. Carlson on his arm.

"My God! Could he have been the guy who…?"

* * *

I hadn't felt this low since my last birthday, so I decided to retreat to my secret place. Every kid I knew had his own secret place—a place where grownups weren't welcome.

Mike's secret place was the outside stairwell which led to his basement. Their TV room was built over this stairwell. Before that time, the stairwell was easily visible from the outside. Afterwards, no one paid attention to the little white door that opened to the stairs leading to the basement. Mike hid there whenever he was in trouble or when we wanted to look at his father's pack of playing cards with a naked woman on each.

Rick, on the other hand, had a serious problem finding a secret place. Seven people lived in his small house, so secret places didn't exist. He cleverly harnessed his greatest skills, taking risks and climbing, and created his handy secret place—any tree that he could climb and he could climb any tree like a squirrel. The question, "Where's Rick?" was commonly answered, "Just look up."

Sometimes we collaborated on a secret place. These collaborative efforts were called "forts," but these were anything but forts, especially if Mike, Rick, and I built them. We gathered scraps of wood, borrowed our dads' tools, and built square structures with a roof and a trap door on top. A less than heavy wind could blow these structures over. Since our families didn't want these unsightly forts marring our backyards, we usually built them in open prairies and vacant lots. Consequently, our forts were constantly invaded by other neighborhood kids when we weren't around. Nevertheless, for a period of time they provided a sanctuary for us to look at dirty pictures, to smoke, to create secret club rituals, or just to be away from the world of grownups.

My secret place was convenient; it was right next to my attic bedroom. The knotty pine paneling extended outside my room along one side of the hallway. The high-pitched roof and the floor created a storage space on the other side of the paneling. The paneling just outside my room was cut into a door with a bar latch; the door opened to the
dirty little storage area with a small dormer built over our front door below. A vent window in the center of the dormer let in some light. The vent window had a thick black screen on the inside and metal shades painted to match the front door just below. A person looking through the vent window from the inside could view all the activities on Glen Lane. A person on the outside looking up at the vent window only saw painted metal shades.

Since my parents stored practically nothing except screens, storm windows, and an old factory fan in this area, it provided a perfect secret place for me. If I rested the factory fan on its side, I could use it as a stool, sit in front of the vent window, and spy on the lane.

Someone had drilled a tiny hole just large enough for a small kid's finger below the door latch. From the inside, I could stick my finger through the hole and lock or unlock the latch.

Many nights when I couldn't sleep or days when I just wanted to be alone, I sat on that large fan and watched the lane. Over time I learned valuable secrets about people on Glen Lane:
While Penny always kissed her dates goodnight by the porch light, Margot always spent at least half an hour in the car with her boyfriends before walking to her doorstep by herself.
Frankie, an eighth-grader, often climbed out his bedroom

window at two in the morning and disappeared into the night. Mr. Stewart, the "health nut" who did jumping jacks on his front lawn every morning, worked the three-to-midnight shift and sat on his front porch after returning from work and drank a pint of whiskey before going into his house. Mr. Carlson worked the night shift and left his house every week night at 11:30 for work. At about 12:15 some guy would knock on the Carlsons' backdoor, and Mrs. Carlson would let him inside. I never learned what time he left.

The Heinz family's lights went off at 9:00 p.m. and back on at 6:00 a.m. They never did anything unusual. Mrs. Sorenson, the old lady who lived in the house at the far end of the lane, walked her dachshund down the lane at 5:00 a.m. She made sure that her dog, Shotsy, crapped on the Carlsons' lawn. Then, she picked out a house with a blossoming flowers out front and dug out a flower to take home.

I knew that all of that gossipy information was of little value to the world beyond Glen Lane. I also knew that to these people these snippets of life were classified secrets. This gave me a needed sense of power, and I declared myself *The King of Glen Lane.*

I sat on the fan, stared out the vent window and tried to think of anything except Little League, but somehow I burst into tears. I cried loud and hard without shame or regard for those 1950s macho standards forced upon me. After a short time, my crying stopped; I didn't try to stop myself...the crying just ended. I felt empty, not good, not bad, not happy, not sad...just empty. Little kids laughed, screamed, and played on the lane as sunrays shot through the clouded sky.

I heard Mom, Big Lou, and Terri enter through the back door. My father must have parked in the alley, so he could haul whatever he had bought into the house. Their presence didn't startle me. Many times I had been in my secret place when the house was full, and no one knew where I was.

This time, however, Big Lou's footsteps clomped up the stairs and down the hallway toward my room. He stopped at the storage room door, worked the latch, and opened it. Before he could store the new storm door he had bought at Sears, he saw me sitting on the fan and staring through the vent window.

"What in the hell?"

He walked the short distance toward me, but I didn't budge or quit staring out the window. I didn't care. He could have yelled at me, interrogated me, even smacked me; I was emotionally drained...I just didn't care.

"Did you hear—"

I looked up at him. When he saw my face, his anger melted. My eyes must have still been red from crying, and my cheeks must have still been tear-stained. I simply said, "I didn't make it."

The look on Big Lou's face was one I had never seen before. It was either pity, empathy, or maybe both. He gently put his hand on my head and silently stared at me for a moment. Then, he said, "This is kind of a dirty place. Better not let your mother know you hang out here."

He quietly walked out and closed the door behind him.

Chapter 33

The following Saturday afternoon I stood in line at Evan's Drug Store to buy a Snickers Bar and a pack of Topps baseball cards…I was celebrating. The previous night a manager called and said that I'd made his Minor Little League Team, the Pirates. To accommodate the massive number of kids who wanted to play baseball, Little League officials had organized two levels: the Little League level and the Minor Little League level. To be on a team at the Little League level, a boy either had to be a "good" player, and/or his dad had to volunteer to be a coach or a manager at that level. To be on a Minor Little League team, a boy had to have a pulse. Since my abilities ranged from "stink" to "almost OK," and Big Lou volunteered to be an umpire, my destiny was to be a Minor Little League player.

That was fine with me; I would be playing baseball.

The line in front of the big pretty lady's cash register was rather long. I amused myself by exploring the magazine rack, an area that I had always ignored. It was a long light pinewood shelving structure that started in the middle of the store at the soda fountain counter and stretched along the east wall to the store's front, a big picture window. Stacks of various newspapers covered the bottom shelf just inches above the floor. Colorful magazines neatly organized in subject areas filled the top shelf. The middle shelf, the comic book section, teased my curiosity. It wasn't as if I had never seen comic books. Beth bought *Archie* and *Betty and Veronica* all the time; however, the glossy action covers of the *Superman* comics intrigued me because I had been a fan of the *Superman* television series starring George Reeves. After leafing through several of them, I made my decision; instead of candy, it would be *Superman* comic books.

Comics were dirt cheap back then, so for the next few weeks I spent my candy and ice cream money on comic books. I became a "Superman aficionado" and learned everything about him from his roots as Superboy to his latent fear of kryptonite. This led me to read comic books about other super heroes such as Batman and the Green Lantern.

One day, I strolled into Evan's to spend more dimes on my *Superman* comic book habit and noticed a few teenage boys looking through a magazine and laughing hysterically. They kept returning to the magazine and laughing again and again. Finally, the cashier lady said gently but firmly, "Gentlemen, if you are going to buy the magazine bring it up to the register. Otherwise, return it to the rack, please."

"Okay," they replied respectfully. They returned it to the rack and left the store.

I had to find out what had tickled those guys so much. I picked up the magazine and stared at the cover. Two things struck me: First, this strange–looking boy, or man, or teen with a head too large for his body, disheveled short reddish hair, and a gapped-tooth smile stared back at me from the page; then, the title of the magazine at the top of the page simply read *Mad*. As I skimmed through it, I realized something was missing—advertising. This "magazine," I thought, was really a cross between a magazine and a comic book. The first section looked like a comic book story, but it was a satire on the current TV cop show *Dragnet*. I read through the story and found myself giggling at the caricatures and the jokes. Scanning further, I laughed out loud at the rather sadistic comic sketch in "The Don Martin Department." I stopped and glanced at the cashier counter. The lady didn't scold me as she did to the teenage guys. She just looked down, smiled, and pretended not to notice me.

Instead of spending my money on several *Superman* comic books, I spent it on *Mad* magazine that day. I read it and shared the humor with my friends. I could hardly wait until the next month's edition was published.

A week later, my trip to Evan's magazine rack took me past the revolving paperback book display. That *Mad* face, that boyish-teenish-adultish ugly face of Alfred E. Newman, grinned at me from the cover of one of those paperbacks. I snatched it from the display and began to skim and scan through it. The *Mad* publisher, William Gaines, published expanded versions of the magazine in paperback format. I returned it to the revolving display because I hadn't enough money and bought my usual *Superman* and *Batman* "literature."

The next week I returned to Evan's, bought the paperback book, *Inside Mad*, and brought it to school the following day.

That second week of June marked the last week of the school year. We were overdue for our final "State-Mandated Air Raid Drill." These mandated drills were a reaction to the Cold War and Khrushchev pounding his shoe on a table in the

U.N. Building and screaming, "We will bury you!" Some psychologists claimed that these air raid drills permanently traumatized young baby boomers, but I don't think so. Most of us didn't even know their meaning until a gifted kid named Walter challenged the system. During our first drill in the fall, we were instructed to crawl under our desks, to fold our bodies over our knees and to cover our eyes; this was called the "duck and cover" position. When the air raid drill siren sounded, everyone in class except Walter assumed the "duck and cover" position. The teacher told Walter to get under his desk, but Walter replied like a miniature scholar, "It's useless; if this were an atomic bomb attack, we'd all die of radiation anyway."

Consequently, the school suspended Walter for making an adult look like a dumb- ass. From then on, we referred to the "duck and cover" position as the "kiss-your-ass-good-bye" position.

While in the kiss-your-ass-good-bye position, I pulled out my copy of *Inside Mad* and secretly read. The first story was a satire of the recent popular horror movie, *The Blob*. Instead of *The Blob*, the story of a gooey jelly-like substance that ate the people in a small town until Steve McQueen and his teen friends figured out a way to stop it, this story was called *The Heap*, a huge smelly mound of garbage that did the same thing as the blob.

Jentz was under his desk, too, right next to mine. "Hey, Jentz," I whispered, "take a look at this." I checked to make sure that the teacher wasn't looking and then slid the book.

He opened it and started to read *The Heap*. Within seconds Jentz let out an uproarious laugh as if he were at recess in the middle of the park. The teacher sprinted down the aisle just as Jentz slid the book back to me.

Jentz was my friend, so I immediately acknowledged ownership of the book and gallantly claimed blame for the disruption. She picked up the book and twisted her face when she saw the cover. She skimmed through it and conducted her one-question interrogation, "Do your parents know you're reading this?"

"I don't know…?"

That was the truth. My parents were content just to see me sitting and reading. I could have been reading a telephone book or a *Playboy* magazine. Nevertheless, if a teacher disapproved of the reading material, they would support her one hundred per cent.

"Well, they're definitely going to know now!" she quipped in her 'gotcha' voice.

"Oh, shit," I mumbled to myself. "This is all I need—Mom and Dad dishing out a punishment just before summer starts!"

She put the copy of *Inside Mad* on the corner of the ink blotter on her desk.

At the end of the school day we stood in two lines (girls in one line, boys in the other) in preparation to march into the hallway and out the main doors at the signal of the bell. The bell rang, and our routine began. When we got into the hallway, however, all hell broke loose. Smitty had had a confrontation during recess with a kid in the third grade. When he saw the kid walking in the hallway from another classroom, something snapped inside of him; he tackled him just inside the main door of the building. Of course all the regimentation broke down as kids ran from their lines to watch the fight. The teachers sprang into action. Some of them ran to break up the fight, while others tried to get us back into lines.

I saw my chance. I ran back into our classroom, grabbed the *Mad* paperback from her desk, hid it under my shirt, and walked past the confusion like I couldn't have cared less, and out the building.

The next day I fully expected to hear about the missing book, so I concocted a story to cover myself, but nothing was said; miraculously, she had forgotten about the whole incident.

"We're going to clean out our desks today, and I'll be collecting and inventorying your textbooks," Miss Lupo said.

I piled my arithmetic book, spelling book, history book, writing book, phonics book, science book, health book, and *Dick and Jane* reader atop my desk.

I was home free.

Chapter 34

I sat on our front porch with a stack of *Superman* comics and *Mad* magazines. The early morning July sun heated the wet lawn and steam rose as if the earth were boiling; however, a cool breeze left over from the evening and the rare absence of children playing on the lane made the front porch a perfect place to read.

The wooden screen door rattled open and slammed shut from the house across the lane. Doug exited his house, crossed over and sat next to me. He was a nineteen-year-old junior college student. In early June he and his parents had moved here from the south side of Chicago. He quickly became very popular with all the neighborhood kids, especially the teenagers. Doug was a handsome, athletic, former streetwise kid who decided to "wise up" and get an education. His olive Italian complexion, short black hair and muscular build made him look "tough." He always walked a little hunched over with a determined expression on his face; his attitude and body language said, "It's time to get down to business." Each weekday he would drive his black and white 1955 Chevy to and from Thornton Junior College in Harvey. His popularity didn't stem from his looks, his athleticism, or even his car. Kids took to Doug because he took the time to throw a baseball or a football around with them, or he'd spend time talking with the teenage kids about their lives and dreams.

I prepared myself for a lecture about my poor taste in reading material; Doug dreamed of becoming an English teacher. To my surprise, he picked up a copy of *Mad* and said, "This is a great example of satire and parody."

Naturally, I knew the meaning of neither satire nor parody, so he had to explain.

He picked up a *Superman* comic, skimmed through it, smiled like he was looking at family photo album, and said, "I remember reading these...great stuff. The Ancient Greeks wrote stories about super heroes. The stories were called Greek myths, but you'll read about mythology in a few years at school."

"Really?"

"Yeah, but if you like action and supernatural stories, there's a book I just read; it's about..." He paused for a moment, looked at me, and shook his head. "Naw, you wouldn't want to read it. It's probably way over your head anyway."

"C'mon! What's it about?"

"Well, it involved these people trying to escape from China during an uprising. They manage to get on a small chartered plane, but they find out that they're being kid- napped. The plane crashes in the middle of the Himalaya Mountains where almost no one had ever been before. It's like a hundred degrees below zero, and they might all freeze to death."

"So, what happens?"

"You sure you want to know?"

"Tell me, damn it!"

"What'd I tell you about swearing? Anyway, they all end up in this place called Shangri-La. In Shangri-La people live to be over two hundred years old, and this high priest, the High Lama, runs the place. The problem is that if someone leaves Shangri-La....Well, you can read it when you're older."

"I want to read it now!"

"It's too hard for you. Besides, you like reading kids' stuff like *Mad* and comic books. If I gave you the book you'd probably read a few paragraphs, set it down, and never look at it again."

"C'mon, Doug! Give me the book! I promise, I'll read it, and you can even give me a quiz on it...no bullshit!"

This time he didn't reprimand me for swearing. He just said, "Okay, but four Saturdays from today, I'm going to give you a quiz on the book. If you don't pass it, you owe me fifty pushups."

Lost Horizon by James Hilton was the first can't-put-this-down novel that I had ever read. Doug was right; the vocabulary was way over my head. I sat with a pocket dictionary next to me as I read day and night whenever I could find the time and a place. It took me over three weeks to read it, and I passed his quiz, too.

From then on, I was hooked on books.

The following Sunday marked my last Minor Little League game of the season. I had one major goal as a Minor Little Leaguer—I wanted to hit a home run. I wanted to know what it felt like when the thickest part of the bat thunked against the ball perfectly and the ball sailed far and high and diminished into a little white pill before disappearing over the chain link fence. Loll had hit two home runs for his Little League team that season.

I just wanted to hit one.

My determination peeked as I stood in the batter's box. I had prepared myself well. I watched and emulated the style of my idol, Ernie Banks. Ernie seemed to hit home runs with artistic ease. He stood in the batter's box, feet apart at just shoulder width and eyes focused straight ahead at the pitcher. His arms, parallel to the ground, stretched straight back from his body. His fingers danced nervously on the neck of the bat as he waited for his pitch. If a pitch dared to pass him waist high over the middle or outside portion of the plate, he fluidly extended his arms, snapped his wrists, and the head of the bat drove the ball cleanly over the ivy-covered wall in Wrigley Field and onto Waveland Avenue.

I had gone to Sunday school *and* church service that day. As I stepped into the batter's box, I looked toward my third-base coach, Mr. Starks. He touched the bill of his cap, wiped his hand across his chest, picked his nose, and put his hands into his pockets. We never knew what in the hell the signals meant, but it was fun to act like a major leaguer staring at his third-base coach and watching the ridiculous pantomimes.

The first pitch was an "Ernie Banks homerun pitch," waist high and just outside the middle of the plate. I swung as hard as I could, but I swung late…Nevertheless, the bat made contact with the ball. A low line drive skidded over the first base bag. The first baseman feebly stabbed at it, but the ball skipped down the right field line toward the fence. The right fielder erroneously thought that I was a "pull" hitter, and he was playing in right-center field.

That's all I saw of the ball and the play. I ran like a rabid rat was chasing me toward second base. As I rounded second Mr. Starks rotated his left arm like a windmill, signaling me to continue toward home plate; but then, he extended his right arm straight forward with his palm up, signaling me to stop. The contradiction of signals didn't bother me; I headed for home! While I rounded third base, the catcher waited for the throw; his eyes moved to the right, so I knew the throw wasn't perfect. With a burst of speed I raced over home plate just as the catcher caught the ball...*way* off-target.

It was like a fairytale ending—not over the fence, but nonetheless, an inside-the-park home run! The crowd, mostly mothers, stood and cheered. I bent over with my hands on my knees, tried to catch my breath, and soaked up the ovation from the stands and from my dugout.

Then, it happened.

As the cheers subsided, I straightened up and walked toward the dugout. Mr. Starks cupped his hands over his mouth and yelled to the scorekeeper, "Give him a triple and an error, Chuck!"

What? A triple and an error! But I had done everything right! I studied and copied Ernie. I went to Sunday school *and* church service. I even made a deal with God: if he would let me hit a homerun on this day, I would stop using swear words.

Son of a bitch.

Chapter 35

Mike and I assumed our traditional Labor Day late afternoon positions; we perched on high sturdy branches of the sour cherry tree in my backyard and gathered handfuls of succulent black-red cherries. Occasionally a September yellow-jacket challenged our modest harvest, but we held our ground and waved it away.

Mike blew out a spray of four or five cherry pits and, perhaps in a moment of *déjà vu*, asked, "Remember when ya' told me all that crap about Clown Town?"

"Yeah." I nodded and shamefully answered, "I remember."

"Why'dja do that, Pudge?"

The Illinois Central commuter train clattered and sparked along the Wentworth railroad tracks only a half block away. The annoying din faded as the train streaked northward toward downtown Chicago, and it left a cold silence that patiently waited for my answer.

"I don't know…I don't know, Mike," was my disappointing answer. "I do know one thing…I'm actually lookin' forward to starting school tomorrow."

Mike looked at me like I had just grown a foot-long beard. He turned his attention back to his handful of cherries, sighed, shook his head, and muttered, "Man, you've changed; you've really changed."

I spat out a mouthful of cherry pits. They sprayed through the shaded air, landed in the tall green tufts of grass, and disappeared.

"I know…I know."

Jentz, Loll, Smitty, Pues, and I were now big-third graders (the top grade at Park School), and we had a brand new teacher. At the end of that first week, we took the traditional reading placement test. I figured that by next week my parents would be notified again that their son was an average-no-significant-gain-from-last-year reader.

The following Monday, the morning bell rang, and we obediently sat in our alphabetical-order-by-last-names seats.

"Louis, will you come to the front of the class, please?"

It was only the second week of school, so I thought, what could I have done? Then I remembered; my teacher from last year was back teaching at Park School. She probably told this new teacher about that stupid *Mad* paperback episode. Shit, lady, let it die!

"Louis, please turn around and face the class. Class, I graded the annual reading placement tests over the weekend. After reviewing the records I noticed that Louis did not show significant reading gains over the years that he has been at Park School. This year, however, his reading scores showed the highest gain over one year that has ever been recorded at Park School. I am singling Louis out because I want all of you to see why the teachers at this school spend so much time emphasizing reading, why it is important that Louis's parents encourage him to read, and why our reading program is so important at this school. Louis, welcome to the 'Alice and Jerry' reading group this year!"

It occurred to me that she had forgotten to credit four significant people: Doug, Superman, Alfred E. Newman, and me. I sat down while the whole class stood up and applauded—not everyone joined the ovation. Jentz, Loll, Smitty, and Pues made faces and booed me, but I expected that; after all, *they* were my friends.

Chapter 36

The gold, red and brown leaves desperately clung to the tree branches as the October breeze swayed the trees back and forth like giant paint brushes against the blue sky. On Saturday mornings during any school year my body robotically ate breakfast, crossed the alley, and entered Mike's backyard through the white picket fence. The cool crisp Indian summer air refreshed me as I walked to his back porch.

Muffled high-pitched whispers came from the direction of the screen door leading to the basement concrete stairwell (Mike's secret place).

I quietly walked to the screen door and peered through it and down the stairwell. At the bottom, Mike and Dwayne huddled in fear at the basement door with a thin cloud of gray smoke rising up the stairs.

"Shit, we're caught!" Dwayne tried to whisper, but his terror raised the volume of his voice.

"No, no," Mike said, "it's just Pudge."

"Whew!" Dwayne exhaled, then commanded, "Well, get down here, idiot, before someone sees ya' talkin' to the door!"

I sensed the atmosphere of espionage, so I opened the rickety screen door like a cat burglar, tiptoed down the stairs, and avoided the clumps of brittle leaves randomly littering the stairwell.

"What the hell are you guys doin'?"

"Dwayne stole this pack of Winstons from his old man's carton."

"Yeah?"

"Yeah, and we're just down here havin' us a smoke," Mike said as if he had been doing this all of his young life.

I had thought that every adult American male was a smoker. In the movies, James Dean and Humphrey Bogart always seemed to be garbling words behind a cigarette dangling between their lips. Even John Wayne smoked. My dad smoked. Mike's dad smoked. Rick's dad smoked. Mr. Stewart, our neighbor who did jumping jacks every morning in his Bermuda shorts and a sleeveless t-shirt, smoked. Most teenagers smoked; they usually smoked non-filter Camels and carried the packs rolled up in the sleeves of their plain white t-shirts.

These smokers often made condescending remarks to kids such as, "This is a filthy habit, kid. Don't get started."

We hated that. It only made us want to smoke more.

"Try one!" Dwayne urged.

"I don't know."

"Cmon, don't be chicken. It's fun!" The excitement in Mike's voice didn't match the look on his face. His eyes looked red and watery, and his face tinged of a strange greenish color.

"Alright, but what do I do?"

Dwayne immediately took the role of my tutor. He took out the opened pack of Winstons from his pocket, turned it upside down, and secured the loose cigarettes with two of his fingers. Next, he gently tapped the pack against the palm of his hand.

"What're ya' doin'?" I asked.

"I don't know, but my old man always does this before he takes one out."

He pointed the pack at me with one cigarette halfway out, and I naively took it out with my thumb and forefinger.

"Okay, now light the end of the cigarette and inhale at the same time."

I was nervous. I wanted to be cool, so I followed his instructions verbatim.

"Put the cigarette in your mouth first, dumb ass!"

Mike shook his head in disbelief.

I put the filter between my lips (at least I did that right). Expertly, I lit the lighter and held the flame to the tip of the cigarette. Nothing seemed to be happening until I followed Dwayne's instructions and sucked in a generous volume of air via the cigarette.

The tip glowed, and I immediately felt a hot airy substance enter my stomach and lungs simultaneously. The substance in my stomach said to my breakfast, "Get out, now!" The substance in my lungs triggered an involuntary cough. The result was that I puked all over Dwayne, the pack of cigarettes, and the Zippo lighter.

I had finally learned to appreciate the joy of smoking.

* * *

Wednesday, 2:15 p.m

  The fresh cool April air greets me like an old friend as I step outside Jenny's Restaurant. Most of the people have left. Dorinda, my two sisters, brothers-in-law, and a few cousins continue reminiscing at a table in the bar.

  My Uncle George stands by his rented car and stares at Holy Sepulcher Cemetery across the street from the parking lot. In his late seventies he represents the sole surviving male sibling of my mother; my father and his five brothers have passed on, also.

  He reaches inside his suit coat pocket and pulls out a big black cigar manufactured in the Florida town where he lives. He bites off the end, spits it out, sticks the narrow end in the center of his mouth, lights the thick end, and then draws the heavy dark smoke into his lungs.

  Damn, I wish he'd quit that filthy habit!

* * *

  Big Lou had been a smoker since he was eighteen. For some reason (work, war, or whatever) his smoking habit had escalated from a pack a day to two-and-a-half packs a day. His chain smoking bothered Mom, but she never said much about it.

  One night after dinner, not long after my first-cigarette fiasco, I surprised myself with some unexpected courage. My father sat across the table from me and lit up his ritualistic after-dinner Salem cigarette, but before he delivered his routine after-dinner family interrogation ("How was school?" etc.), the words erupted from me, "Dad, why do you smoke? It's a filthy habit. You never should've started."

Mom couldn't withhold her gasp, and she started removing glassware from the table just in case Big Lou unleashed with one of his famous over-the-table slaps. Beth closed her eyes tightly in preparation for the explosion. Toddler Terri didn't know what the hell was going on and continued to try to find her mouth with a handful of Jell-O.

He gave me a long wide-eyed gaze across the table. His expression, however, was not the usual one of his slowly building anger. His stare reflected a deep introspective moment. After several long minutes, he stood up, extinguished the flame of his cigarette in his mashed potatoes, took his pack of Salems from his shirt pocket, and quietly walked past me to the bathroom.

A plunking sound echoed from the bathroom as he dropped each cigarette, one by one, into the toilet bowl water. After flushing the toilet, he returned to the table and sat down again.

"So how was school?" he asked.

He never smoked again.

Chapter 37

Winter rudely stormed into Chicago early, the week before Thanksgiving. The temperature dropped below freezing for several days, and the wind angled snow flurries toward the ground where they disappeared like magic dust. My baseball buddies, a few other guys, and I stood around the playground during recess with our hands in our pockets and pretended that the mist from our breath was cigarette smoke.

"You guys don't get it," Walter continued. "The way a woman gets pregnant is that when a man and a woman hold hands the sweat gets mixed together and goes into the woman's body and—"

Smitty honked a loud laugh and Pues joined with his deep aristocratic, "*He-Ha!*"

"Where'd you get that!" Pues mocked. "She gets pregnant when they kiss and swap spit."

I didn't dare offer my limited knowledge. The closest Big Lou ever came to talking to me about sex was when he gave me my first jockstrap and said, "Wear this whenever you play sports. It'll protect your testicles. You're gonna' need 'em later."

"For what?" I asked.

"Never mind."

Case closed.

I asked my mother, "Where do babies come from?"

She replied, "Ask your dad."

When I told her about his jockstrap speech she rolled her eyes and sighed. Then, she thought for a moment, took off her apron, and sat me down at the kitchen table.

"When two people fall in love," she began like a Sunday school teacher, "they get married. Then, God plants a little seed…"

Even a little kid recognizes the pungent smell of bullshit. Nevertheless, I respectfully listened, nodded, and then went off to play.

Mike's dad delivered a much better formal lecture. Mike confided the highlights of the "birds and the bees" speech.

"First," he said, "Dad said that we use our penises to have babies."

"Yeah?"

"Yeah."

"How?"

"I don't know, but he said sometimes when we think about girls or when we wake up in the morning, it's real hard and straight."

"Yeah?"

"Yeah."

That still left a big gaping hole in the answer. We decided to take our questions to the ultimate source, Jentz. Jentz knew an older kid who lived down the alley from him. We never knew his real name, but Jentz had nicknamed him "Chopper." According to Jentz, Chopper told him the whole story of where babies come from. The information, however, was classified, and Jentz was sworn to secrecy.

We told Jentz what Mike's dad had told him, and we asked him what it meant. He said he'd check it out with Chopper.

A few days later he confided, "Chopper said that the hard-on-in-the-morning thing your old man's talkin' about is called *morning rod*."

Morning rod, I thought, sounds like something from a poem, but we still didn't know what that had to do with having babies.

Chucky, a tall lanky youth, broke in, "You mean if a guy holds hands with a girl and kisses her at the same time he's sure to get her pregnant?"

All the while, Jentz listened and grew angrier and angrier. He had been rolling his eyes and shaking his head after hearing each theory. Finally, he couldn't take anymore. His classified information from Chopper went public.

"You dumb shits!" he screamed. "Don't you get it? It's not about spit and sweat. If you want to make a baby you have *got* to pee inside the place where she pees!"

Silence.

There was nothing more to say.

Chapter 38

Jentz and I had become close friends since the start of the school year. Mike and I remained best friends, but once school started, we each gravitated more toward kids in our own class. The irony was that Jentz and I were opposites. He was a White Sox fan; I was a Cub fan. He was stocky, strong, and moved slowly; I was thin, wiry, and fast. We both loved sports, but Jentz would spend hours trying to emulate the Ted Williams batting stance; I would have rather read a book or seen a movie about his life.

Jentz and his family lived in an old four-flat apartment building across from the huge park behind Park School. His younger brother, a smaller replica of Jentz himself, didn't escape his older brother's gift for handing out nicknames. Jentz nicknamed him Lumpy after a character of the same name on *Leave It To Beaver*. Their mother, a tall thin woman with a handsomely chiseled face, treated Jentz's and Lumpy's friends like her own sons. She always seemed happy and busy. The father worked hard and long hours at the filling station he owned on the eastern border of Riverdale. In those days nearly every gas station was also an auto repair shop. He was a big man with thinning brown hair, and he would give Jentz and me quarters to clean the gas pump windows and to do other odd jobs around the station. I didn't know much about him except that Jentz thought the world of him.

The week after Thanksgiving we were granted a day off school for a Teachers' Institute Day; the teachers had to attend school, and we didn't. Jentz and I planned to ride the commuter train that day to downtown Chicago, look at the Christmas decorations, and just goof around. There were two ways to execute our plan: We could ask permission from our parents and risk being told, "No, you're too young!" or we could sneak downtown and risk getting caught and punished. Although the latter would have been much more exciting, we knew that the chances of getting caught were extremely high since many adults who rode the commuter train to work knew our parents and gladly would have snitched on us. Our parents surprisingly thought our plan was a great idea. They said it would be a good life experience and secretly told their commuter friends to keep an eye on us. My mother bought the train tickets and instructed us on their use. Mrs. Jentz drew a map of the downtown streets and highlighted points of interest.

We had a fantastic time. We sat on the oily wicker seats of the train, laughed and joked about the serious-looking commuters. We befriended a homeless guy, Jacob, who begged in the tunnel leading under Michigan Avenue from the train station to Randolph Street. Jacob pretended to be blind as he sat in the tunnel with his old German shepherd, Ulysses, and rattled a tin can full of coins and bills. "Cheap fucker, don't he know it's Christmas," he sputtered after someone dropped a dollar bill instead of a five in his cup and walked away. The ninety-foot real Christmas tree in Marshall Field's restaurant brought thousands of tourists to Chicago.

The colored lights, shiny huge ornaments, and sheer massiveness of the tree amazed us. We ate at a famous hamburger joint called *Wimpy's* on Wabash Street.

We saved the best place for last—the indoor carnival store on Randolph Street that Mike and I had visited when J.P. brought us downtown. Pinball machines, bowling machines, and ring toss kept us busy for about an hour.

The next train left for the south suburbs about a half hour later. We killed time in a little novelty gift shop next door. The store featured gag gifts, cards, and posters; naked pictures of women with crude captions signaled that we probably shouldn't have been in there. One eight-by-ten poster doubled us over with laughter. It pictured a wrinkled smiling old geezer with a piece of chewing tobacco dripping from his mouth. He was dressed in a U.S. Air Force test pilot uniform—helmet and all. The caption below the picture read: *Sleep tight tonight. Your Air Force is awake.*

Jentz bought the poster, vowed to hide it in his school folder, and crack people up during class.

Max, the janitor, plopped his dirty stringy mop on the tile floor in the front of the classroom. Miss Lindsay, our third-grade teacher, had tried to show us the power of air pressure during our science lesson. She filled an empty gallon paste jar with water and put a piece of cardboard over the top.

"When I, with the help of these two volunteers, turn the jar over, the air pressure, pushing up on the piece of cardboard, will hold all this water in the jar."

Loll produced a mock drum roll by pounding his palms on his desktop.

They turned the paste jar over.

The air pressure lost.

It was Wednesday, the third week in December. Our two-week holiday break started after school on Friday, so everyone was a little excited and less than studious. The chatter and laughter created a party-like atmosphere that Miss Lindsay wisely didn't challenge. From the back of the room Jentz held up the *Your Air Force is Awake* poster, and I surrendered to a boisterous belly laugh.

Outside our warm classroom, the thick snowflakes that once disappeared into the warm earth now settled and stayed on the cold pavement and grass. Max shook his head at the shoveling project that was building outside for him as he left our classroom with the filthy wet mop balanced over his shoulder.

A green and white '54 Chevy Belair cut through the thin blanket of snow on the circular drive and parked by the curb near the main entrance. A woman wearing a navy blue hooded wool winter coat hurriedly exited from the driver's-side door and scurried inside the building. She came straight to our classroom and approached Miss Lindsay. When the woman flipped off the hood with a toss of her head, I recognized her; it was Jentz's Aunt Rose. She whispered a few sentences to Miss Lindsey who produced a painful look on her face and mouthed words that seemed to say, "I am so sorry."

Jentz with a confused expression on his face approached his aunt. She instructed him to get his coat and hat and to meet her in the car. After a short conversation with Miss Lindsey, Jentz's aunt scurried back to the car and drove away with Jentz in the front seat.

Everyone in class wondered what was going on, but Miss Lindsay refused to say anything and told us to get out our arithmetic books. I figured that Jentz had a dentist or doctor appointment and his mom had forgotten to tell him. Anyway, I'd call him after school and find out.

When I got home from school, my mother sat at the kitchen table with her head in her hands. Through a sorrowful expression, she simply and softly stated, "Jentz's dad passed away suddenly; they think it was a brain tumor."

Her expression yielded to worry. Knowing how death could traumatize me, she probably worried about how this news would affect me. I, however, wasn't thinking about death; I was thinking about my buddy—Jentz.

My parents took me to the wake Friday night. He was waked at the Community Mortuary, only a few blocks from his filling station. Friends and relatives packed the funeral home. A line that nearly went out the doors into the cold snowy air moved slowly through the lobby and toward the chapel room. We moved inside the chapel doors, and my eyes busily searched for Jentz within the crowded ornate room. With only a few groups of mourners ahead of us, the shiny brown coffin emerged surrounded by colorful standing flower arrangements and banners.

Jentz's dad lay peacefully in the white cushy lined coffin. Nothing about his appearance in that coffin (the peaceful expression, the glasses, the white starched shirt, silk tie, the dark business suit) reminded me of him in life. In life his face reflected his work—the strain, the determination, and the fatigue; his work shirt, stained and scented with the gas, oil, grease, and cigar smoke, fit him perfectly, and the rolled-up sleeves revealed his manly forearms.

A small cluster of people walked from the coffin, and Mrs. Jentz stood alone and sported a warm brave smile, but her eyes couldn't mask her weariness. She held out her arms. "Elsie, Lou, and my good buddy!" she quietly exclaimed and gave each of us a hug.

She and my parents chit-chatted a short while. Then, Big Lou asked, "Where are the boys?"

"It's been a long day for both of them. They're taking it pretty hard, so I sent them home with Rose and Dick."

I was both sad and relieved. I wanted to let my buddy know that I was sorry. At the same time, I didn't know what I could say to him that would help in any way; he truly loved and admired his dad.

Big Lou pushed against the heavy glass door that the strong, cold wind sealed shut. We stepped from the thick-carpeted, parlor-furnished lobby of the funeral home and into the dark freezing cold of the living.

I awoke early the next morning and started my Saturday morning ritual. Everyone still slept, so I made my bowl-of-*Cheerios*-glass-of-orange-juice breakfast and sat at the kitchen table.

Outside, a light thick coat of virgin snow covered the backyard and every branch of the cherry tree. A bird landed on a thin branch near the kitchen window. Its landing cleared a small patch of snow from the branch, so the bird nestled between the two white walls. It had an orange breast; it was a robin!

I marveled at its existence in this early Chicago winter. Robins allegedly signaled the coming of spring. Perhaps this robin was sick and couldn't make the trip south to warmer states, and yet it looked healthy and well fed. In fact, this robin cocked its head and stared at me through the glass as if *I* were out of place!

The bird hopped and turned away from me; it landed exactly on the bare spot of the branch that it had cleared on its original landing. Using the bobbing of the branch, the robin sprang into the air and flew southward. The thin branch vibrated like a diving board after a strong athletic diver has launched a graceful and spectacular maneuver. The vibrations shook the airy white snow from the branch and left it wet, naked, and healthy; the branch appeared as if it would miraculously sprout dark green leaves and bright red cherries at any moment.

That's when it hit me—no nightmares...no terrifying images of Mr.Charleston, my grandfather, Mary or tragic deaths.

I ravenously gulped down the last of my orange juice and let some of the sweet nectar drip from the corners of my mouth.

Chapter 39

"Hey, Big Jim, are those your men?"

"Hey, Ray!" I stood up from the living room floor where Mike, Rick, and I had been playing *Clue* and greeted him and Dorothy at the front door. Beth, her long brown ponytail bobbing with each step, had run downstairs when she heard the doorbell ring and let them in. She and some of her neighborhood friends were upstairs playing records, talking, and babysitting three-year-old Terri for the night.

"We'll take your coats. Go on downstairs," Beth instructed. "Mom, Dad, and everyone are down there."

Beth carefully helped Dorothy, who was pregnant again, with her coat. They had dropped off Cindy, their first-born, with my grandparents in Harvey; the side trip and heavy snow had made them late for my parents' New Year's Eve party .

I took Ray's heavy black leather motorcycle jacket and put it on. The sight of me wearing that huge thing on my little body cracked everyone up.

"Maybe in a few years, Big Jim," Ray said and led Dorothy downstairs. "Take care, men!"

"See ya!" Mike and Rick said in unison.

When I returned from tossing the leather coat on my parents' bed atop the pile of other winter coats, Rick asked, "Who's that guy? He's cool."

"That's my Uncle Ray."

"What's with that 'Big Jim' stuff?" Mike asked.

"Aw, he just calls me that. My middle name is James."

"That's cool too!" Rick added. "That's your new name now—Jim!"

And so ended *Pudge, Pudgie, Louis* and the 1950s.

* * * *

Ray would continue his wild ways—drinking, chasing women—and it put a heavy strain on his health and marriage; nevertheless, Dorothy and Ray stayed together and raised three more boys after Cindy. The middle son enlisted in the marines after high school and became an honor guard for President Reagan. While stationed in Washington D.C., he wanted to own a motorcycle, just like his dad in his younger days. Ray sent him the money. On a rainy warm summer night, he lost control of the bike on an overpass, crashed into the guardrail, and fell to his death on the pavement below.

Ray never forgave himself.

Several changes rocked Mike's life in the early 1960s: Marion gave birth to a girl; Mickey got transferred, and the family moved to Louisville, Kentucky where Mike lived until he finished high school. He continued on to college and medical school. Mike currently practices at the prestigious MAYO Clinic in Jacksonville, Florida. Our strong friendship has endured over the years, but as in many friendships, our contact has been reduced to calls and cards on birthdays and holidays only.

Rick survived the "Dare-Devil Rick" days of his youth. He has worked as a chemist for some major corporations in the Chicago area. Some forty-plus years after that New Year's Eve party, a deep but familiar voice from the end of a bar where I was celebrating with friends summoned, "Hey, Pudgie!" In the dim smoky light of the tavern, Rick appeared unchanged from the exuberant youthful boy I remembered. We spent hours recreating moments from our past and let time do its magic with exaggeration and fabrication.

Beth, Terri, and I followed a similar pattern. We worked in schools: I taught high school English classes; they worked as social workers. All three of us are married and still live in the Chicago area. We stay in close contact.

Big Lou struggled over the next forty years. He survived a series of heart attacks beginning in 1967. The heart attacks didn't hurt him as much as that "wild animal" inside of him. He never learned to release his strong emotions and fought hard to control them and to keep them hidden inside. The "wild animal" beat him up from within and left him weak and vulnerable. He died of complications due to heart disease in 1988.

Mom commanded the position of family matriarch for fifty-six years. She settled family squabbles, lent and gave money, traveled, and kept in contact with relatives and friends until cancer took her down in 2002; even cancer had a tough time.

* * * *

The lights were off, but the room brightened and dimmed to the light of the TV screen. Rick dozed in Big Lou's lounge chair. Mike and I rested our heads on the pillows at the opposite ends of our living room couch that faced the TV. In Riverdale it was only eleven o'clock, but in New York, where Jack Paar hosted *The Tonight Show*, midnight had just arrived. The broadcast switched from the NBC studios to Times Square. 1959 diminished in New York with fireworks on the TV screen mixed with the muffled sounds of the party in the basement below us.

My drowsiness wouldn't yield to sleep, and I tried in vain to enjoy the colorful fireworks on our black-and-white TV screen. I closed my eyes and turned on my imagination...The fireworks display looked like tiny embers of tobacco bouncing off our concrete porch steps from Big Lou's fallen cigarette.

Epilogue

Thursday, 1:20 a.m.

I'm alone in my sanctuary—my basement bar. My basement immortalizes the 1950s. The 1950s die-cast car collection covers the finished pine case along the basement wall on the other side of the bar. A die-cast '57 Belair, red body, white top, two-door Chevy and a picture/plaque of the same highlight the display. Shiny trophies stand tall at each end of the die-cast car display. The trophies belong to the real '57 Chevy that beauty-sleeps under a protective cover in my garage.

My pride in the '57 Chevy does not come from the restoration trophies it has earned. My pride in the car came last summer when I drove my newly restored '57 Chevy to show my Uncle Ray. He and Dorothy live in Frankfort, Illinois, not far from the place where Ray took me on that wild ride in his '57 Chevy so many years ago. Ray's body is now crippled from the effects of diabetes and his years of fast living. His mind suffers from periods of dementia, also. When I helped his tortured body in his walker toward the front door, a wide grin illuminated his face as my car came into view. I dared not interrupt his precious thoughts. Was he thinking of his own '57 Chevy? Did he realize that my car symbolized all the things he had done for me in my youth?

I don't know.

Many tributes to James Dean array the basement in the forms of framed photos, posters, tin signs, a Christmas ornament, refrigerator magnets, a clock, and even two life-size cardboard cutouts of him. Many people, who normally consider me to be sane and level-headed, challenge their own judgment when they see my tribute to him; I can't testify to my own sanity. Perhaps the brevity of his life reminds me of the brevity of mine. Maybe he represents all the lessons about death that I learned as a child in the darkness of the movie theaters or the cruel indiscriminate nature of death itself.

Again, I really don't know.

The most poignant picture in this basement museum hangs on the narrow finished pine partition at the far end of the bar. It's a picture that I ruined circa 1953. Mom was trying to take a picture of my father, his four surviving brothers, and my grandfather (my father's father). The theme was similar to that of a team picture. My father and two of his brothers were on one knee facing the camera. My grandfather and the other two brothers stood behind them. Each man held a bottle of Schlitz beer as they posed. Just before Mom clicked the camera shutter, a little curly-haired toddler walked into the left corner of the frame, took a bottle from his Uncle Joe's hand, put its mouth to his lips, and chugged it down. All six men looked at the intruder and burst into laughter.

Mom snapped the picture.

On the counter case beyond the 1950s die-cast cars and beyond the trophies, a seven-foot mirror stretches from one end of the counter case to the other. My image seated at the bar with a half-full bottle of Miller Lite beer resting on the bar with my hand encircling it reflects back to me.

I glance back at that 1953 team beer-drinking picture again.

I guess I really haven't ventured very far from Riverdale or that picture over the past fifty years or so...or have I?

A moment of clairvoyance leads to a long silence. I am caught in an inexplicable deep introspection. I close my eyes so my imagination can color this dream—I am in my attic bedroom writing in the spiral notebook atop my built-in desk:

The fear of death follows from the fear of life.

A man who lives fully is prepared to die at any time.

Mike, I think there really is a *Clown Town*. I think that I have created it, after all.

Acknowledgements

I extend a literary thank-you to John McNally, Tom Jenks, Chris Noel, Tony Ardizzone, Jill Pollack and the Story Studio gang, Mitch Markovitz (illustrator), and Dorinda (my wife and editor-in-chief).

A heartfelt thank-you goes to Beth, Terry, Mike, Rick, and Riverdale.

Printed in the United States
117904LV00001B/1/P

9 781598 586374